Piracy in the Early Modern Era

An Anthology of Sources

Piracy in the Early Modern Era

An Anthology of Sources

Edited and translated,
with an Introduction, by
Kris Lane and Arne Bialuschewski

Hackett Publishing Company, Inc.
Indianapolis/Cambridge

22 21 20 19   1 2 3 4 5 6 7

For further information, please address
Hackett Publishing Company, Inc.
P.O. Box 44937
Indianapolis, Indiana 46244-0937

www.hackettpublishing.com

Cover design by Rick Todhunter
Interior design by Laura Clark
Composition by Aptara, Inc.

Library of Congress Cataloging-in-Publication Data

Names: Lane, Kris E., 1967– editor. | Bialuschewski, Arne.
Title: Piracy in the early modern era : an anthology of sources /
    edited and translated, with an introduction, by Kris Lane and Arne
    Bialuschewski.
Description: Indianapolis : Hackett Publishing Company, Inc., 2019. |
    Includes bibliographical references and index.
Identifiers: LCCN 2019020340| ISBN 9781624668258 (cloth) |
    ISBN 9781624668241 (pbk.)
Subjects: LCSH: Pirates—History—Sources. |
    Piracy—History—Sources.
Classification: LCC G535 .P483 2019 | DDC 364.16/4—dc23
LC record available at https://lccn.loc.gov/2019020340

∞

ACKNOWLEDGMENTS

We would like to acknowledge the following individuals for supporting this project: our editor Rick Todhunter, the anonymous readers for Hackett Publishing, Marc Eagle, Mark Hanna, Raynald Laprise, David Wilson, and Kate Zubczyk. Financial support was provided by the School of Liberal Arts at Tulane University, and the Social Sciences and Humanities Research Council of Canada.

CONTENTS

CHRONOLOGY

1453	Ottomans take Constantinople
1492	Columbus reaches Caribbean
1494	Treaty of Tordesillas between Spain and Portugal
1504	Oruç Barbarossa takes papal galleys off Civita Vecchia (near Rome)
1517	Oruç Barbarossa defeats Spanish fleet off Algiers, dies in 1518 battle
1522	Suleiman the Magnificent's forces capture Rhodes from Knights of St. John
1523	Jean Florin captures portion of Cortés' treasure off Portugal
1527	Ottoman corsairs defeat Portuguese to control Yemeni entrance to Red Sea
1528	First recorded pirate attack in the Caribbean
1529	Hayreddin Barbarossa drives Spanish from fort off Algiers
1536	Unknown French corsair attacks north coast of Panama
1538	First pirate attack on the city of Havana
1543	Seignieur de Roberval sacks towns on north coast of Colombia
1545	"Pirate king" Wang Zhi moves to southwest Japan
1546	Hayreddin Barbarossa dies; Portuguese capture Basra: Ottomans fail to take Diu
1551	Turgut Reis (Dragut) takes Tripoli from Knights of Malta
1552	Portuguese defeat Ottomans at Hurmuz
1553	Henri II of France authorizes corsair attacks in Caribbean
1554	Jacques Sores raids Santiago de Cuba
1555	Sores sacks Santa Marta (Colombia) and Havana
1556	Ottoman corsair Sefer Reis raids coast of India
1559	Treaty of Cateau-Cambrésis ends French war with Spain; China's "pirate king" Wang Zhi executed by Ming authorities

1561	Spain creates formal transatlantic fleet system to protect valuables
1562	First contraband slaving voyages of John Hawkins to Caribbean; French attempt to create corsair base in northern Florida under Jean Ribault
1564	Second Hawkins slaving voyage to Caribbean; second and third French Huguenot expeditions to Florida; Sefer Reis raids Africa's Swahili Coast
1565	Menéndez Avilés destroys French outposts in Florida
1566	Francis Drake and John Lovell attempt contraband trade on Venezuelan coast
1567	Drake and Hawkins' third slaving voyage to Caribbean, punished by Spanish fleet at San Juan de Ulúa (Veracruz, Mexico) in 1568
1571	Don Juan of Austria leads Christian allies in defeat of Ottoman forces at Lepanto
1572	Drake returns to Caribbean, attacks Panama treasure house
1574	Limahon (Lin Feng) attacks Manila; Uluç Ali Pasa captures La Goletta fortress
1575	Miguel de Cervantes captured by corsairs, taken to Algiers
1577–1580	Drake's circumnavigation, includes capture of prize *Cacafuego* off Peru (1579)
1584	First expedition by Walter Raleigh to Virginia
1586	Drake returns to Caribbean, captures Santo Domingo, Cartagena; Mir Ali Beg raids Swahili coast
1587	Thomas Cavendish takes Manila galleon near Baja California
1588	Anglo-Dutch defeat of Spain's invincible Armada
1594–1595	Hawkins' ill-fated South Sea voyage ends with capture off Ecuador
1595	Last Drake expedition to Caribbean ends in his death off Panama (1596)
1598	George Cumberland attacks Puerto Rico; death of Philip II of Spain
1599	Portuguese attack Malabar to punish corsairs
1600	Olivier van Noort enters Spanish Pacific

1603	Death of Elizabeth I; peace with Spain under James I (1604)
1605	Spanish attack Dutch salt gatherers at Punta de Araya in Venezuela
1609	Start of Twelve Years Truce between Spain and Netherlands
1615	Joris van Speilbergen destroys Spanish fleet off coast of Peru
1617–1618	Raleigh's disastrous El Dorado expedition
1621	End of Twelve Years Truce, Dutch found West India Company
1624	Dutch attack Peru coast, capture Bahia, Brazil; Dutch drive Spanish from Taiwan
1628	Piet Heyn captures New Spain silver fleet at Matanzas Bay, Cuba; pirate Zheng Zhilong joins Ming forces
1629	Cornelis Jol (Pie de Palo) fails to take Havana, joined by Diego el Mulato
1633	Cornelis Jol and Diego el Mulato take Campeche
1634	Dutch establish contraband base at Curaçao
1635	Spanish drive early raiders from Tortuga (off Hispaniola)
1641	Spanish drive Puritans from Providence Island
1642	William Jackson sacks Maracaibo, Venezuela
1648	Peace of Münster ends war between Spain and the Netherlands
1654	Dutch driven from northeast Brazil
1655	English take Jamaica after failure at Santo Domingo
1659	Christopher Myngs destroys Cumaná, Venezuela
1661	Koxinga (Cheng Chenggong) defeats Dutch at Taiwan
1662	Myngs takes Santiago de Cuba
1663	Myngs sacks Campeche
1665	Buccaneers sack Granada, Nicaragua
1666	François L'Olonnais takes Maracaibo and Gibraltar
1667	Henry Morgan attacks Puerto Príncipe
1668	Morgan seizes Portobelo, Panama
1669	Morgan takes Maracaibo and Gibraltar
1670	Treaty of Madrid establishes peace between England and Spain
1671	Morgan pillages Panama City

MAPS AND IMAGES

GENERAL INTRODUCTION

Piracy, or armed robbery at sea, is an ancient phenomenon, and yet it remains poorly understood. Were all pirates criminals? When was piracy warfare by other means? When was it rebellion against oppressive forces? Were victims of seaborne marauders right to call their attackers pirates? How did pirates differ from corsairs or privateers? Who joined the pirates? Were pirate crews typically diverse or homogeneous? What role did religion play in the global history of piracy? Were there pirate subcultures or even pirate nations? Why did piracy rise and fall in cycles, and where was it most common? Did pirates write about their exploits, and if so, why and for whom?

As it happens, some pirates *did* write about their experiences, but more often we learn about them from their victims and enemies. The same could be said of land-based robbers, including those who, like Robin Hood, were celebrated for challenging corrupt officials or unfair laws. Feared for their mobility and admired for their audacity, the pirates of the early modern era (c.1450–1750) grabbed the attention of increasingly literate populations worldwide, even as they filled readers' or listeners' minds with horror and fascination. Contemporaneous writings by and about pirates ranged from memoirs to legal treatises to sworn testimonies to sermons, extending into other genres such as poetry and song. People who could not read about pirates heard of their exploits from travelers, preachers, town criers, balladeers, and playwrights.

The truth about piracy has thus been varnished over the years, and many legends and myths have arisen. To get closer to the truth about piracy, one must examine as many sources as possible. Best are those produced during the pirates' lifetimes, and better yet is an assembly that provides multiple angles or perspectives on a particular pirate or pirate subculture.

Nothing is transparent, of course, and all sources have their biases. As with the history of crimes and misdemeanors more generally, one must read between the lines and check sources against one another since acts of piracy were rarely recorded dispassionately. What makes pirate-related documents yet more difficult is their typically cross-cultural nature, shot through with linguistic, religious, national, and other differences. Even so, the overwhelming majority of surviving sources on piracy were written and consumed by Europeans or their colonial offspring. In lieu of major archival discoveries, a truly global history of piracy remains difficult to construct.

Before diving into a sampling of pirate records, it may be useful to review some high points in the history of piracy during the early modern period and also to summarize key models and broader scholarly approaches to the topic. Next is a review of terminology, in part because insults and euphemisms were frequently used to describe sea raiders, depending on the writer's or witness' perspective. Last is a brief discussion of surviving sources and how they were generated, used, and preserved.

Piracy: Ancient to Modern

As a simple act of robbery at or by descent from the sea, piracy may be about as old as humankind. Yet historians tend to associate sea bandits with expanding maritime empires and sometimes with internal social conflict. Even the ancient Egyptians recorded attacks on their merchant vessels by violent "sea peoples," but the Egyptians were not famed for their maritime exploits or overseas claims. Other victims who left no written records likely suffered seaborne attacks well before the Egyptians, yet we know little about them beyond archaeological or artistic traces.

Sea raiders were found in many other parts of the ancient world, particularly in heavily traversed sea-lanes such as those of southeast Asia or the Arabian Sea connecting Africa to the Middle East and South Asia. Merchant vessels tended to follow known routes and to rely on currents and seasonal winds, so pirates knew where to lie in wait and when to attack. Estuaries, straits, and other choke points were choice locations. Some sea raiders were a chronic hazard, whereas others appeared and disappeared in line with increasing or decreasing opportunities. Still other piratical cultures were suppressed by well-organized victims, but this was rare.

Sea raiding appears to have been ancient in the Caribbean Sea and in much of the vast Pacific Ocean basin as well, oftentimes as an extension of vengeance cycles and frequently charged with religious meaning. We know most about these kinds of raids, usually centered on captive taking, from modern ethnographic evidence, although archaeology has been helpful. Modern accounts suggest that prehistoric Polynesian and

Micronesian sea raiding bore a resemblance to the raids carried out by the famous Caribs for whom the Caribbean was named.

Capturing live human beings was the main objective for many of the world's sea-roving peoples, a theme familiar to the Greeks of Homer's day. One difference was that Pacific raiders traversed far greater distances than those of either their Caribbean or Mediterranean counterparts, requiring more sophisticated vessels and stellar navigation techniques. Whether or not these various non-literate island or seafaring cultures had a term equivalent to the Greek *peirates*, or "sea bandit" (the root of the Western word "pirate") ancient sea raiding probably felt like piracy to its victims no matter where they lived.

We know that piracy flourished in the Mediterranean until the Roman imperial age, when Pompey the Great and others launched massive suppression campaigns, giving rise to the ideal of the *Mare Nostrum* or controlled sea. The famous Roman orator Cicero made a name for himself as an enemy of pirates, which he saw as a threat to the republic. Before this novel claim of the sea or of major waterways as sovereign space, it was catch as catch can, and glory to the gods if one arrived at one's destination with person, ship, and cargo intact. With the decline of Rome, piracy again surged, both in the Mediterranean and in the North Atlantic. In northern and western Europe, the Vikings added terror to the many hazards of the Middle Ages by plundering at sea, and some Norse raiding expeditions reached the Mediterranean.

By late-medieval times the Vikings began to retreat or settle down as colonists, and Mediterranean piracy in particular became more or less formalized, often tied to religious strife as well as to merchant expansion and the rise of regional commercial bases and city-states such as Venice, Ragusa, Genoa, Barcelona, Smyrna, and Cairo. The Mamluks extended their commercial influence and political power into the Red Sea and beyond, but without establishing Roman-style sea hegemony. The upstart Ottomans who displaced the Mamluks came closer to achieving this objective in the sixteenth century, yet Persian Gulf raiders remained a menace, alternately fishing for pearls and looting stray ships.

Aside from crusading expeditions, which had religious aims beyond pillage, very long-distance pirate raids were rare in the late-medieval West, and no empire dominated western seas. To paraphrase the great sociologist Max Weber, no state or sovereign had a monopoly on the legitimate use of violence within the Mediterranean trading sphere. Even so, merchant cities with powerful navies and increasingly sophisticated gunpowder weapons, such as Venice and Genoa, used deadly force when harassed by sea bandits. As in Roman times, however, fighting pirates "at their nests" was expensive and rarely had lasting effects. The Uskoks of Senj, a sea bandit culture on the Adriatic's Dalmatian coast, were a chronic thorn in Venice's side.

Piracy surged in eastern seas in early modern times, particularly along the monsoon trade circuit linking Africa and Arabia to India and southeast Asia. Bandits emerged in places such as Oman and Bahrain as mercantile sea traffic exploded in volume. Were there always pirates here or was this a new phenomenon, a response to European monopoly claims? Historians disagree about the relationship between piracy and global imperial expansion. Several scholars have argued that piracy as we know it was a side effect or even direct product of western European incursions in Afro-Asian waters, and that peaceful trade was generally practiced in this broad zone before about 1500.

Evidence of piracy from before the era of European expansion into Asia is arguably ambiguous. The famous long-distance voyages of the Ming mariner Zheng He (c.1415–1425) produced intriguing narratives, suggesting to modern readers that he suppressed pirates in the Malacca Strait before going on to India and East Africa. Western translators of Ming chronicles have used the term "pirate" to describe a local chieftain known as Chen Zui, whom Zheng He ordered executed for alleged extortion and other crimes, but there is debate about what legal principles might have been at play.[1] Was Chen Zui a pirate or just a powerful local lord who got in Zheng He's way?

As Anthony Reid notes, the Chinese terms *haizei* ("sea bandit"), *haikou* ("sea traitors"), and *wokou* ("dwarf bandit") were applied by Ming writers and officials in distinct ways. The first two types were classed as rogue Ming subjects who robbed other Ming subjects at sea or onshore and the third were alleged foreigners, typically labeled Japanese although most were not. Ming and Qing officials routinely demonized anyone who robbed at sea or who traded outside the official system, often conflating contraband trade with theft. But according to Reid, this was done without a notion of piracy as a specific class of crime, or of the pirate as a specific type of criminal. The problem, says Reid, is that European scholars have been too quick to call these various lawbreakers pirates, when the

---

1. Jennifer L. Gaynor, "Piracy in the Offing: The Law of Lands and the Limits of Sovereignty at Sea," *Anthropological Quarterly* 85:3 (Summer 2012): 817–57.

term is freighted with Western social, legal, and historical assumptions.[2] Put another way, Reid sees Chen Zui as a pirate only in translation. Were Asian, Arabian, and East African fishing cultures, monsoon traders, and other local seafarers and their land-based sponsors simply relabeled as "pirates" by monopoly-oriented Europeans? This was probably true in many cases, especially when it served imperial interests, yet it appears that some fishermen and petty traders reacted to harsh European actions by turning pirate, that is, by taking up sea raiding as a new if not permanent livelihood. Oppression could breed resistance in this form, particularly in hard times. The same was true of certain marginalized subjects of Western states and empires, usually labeled castaways, renegades, or traitors, leading several historians to characterize piracy as a form of class warfare or "social banditry." In all these cases piracy is seen as a kind of revenge.

Charges of piracy or at least sea banditry flew throughout the early sixteenth century along China's Fujian coast, partly inspired by Portuguese incursions in Melaka and elsewhere, but more driven by conflicts over trade with Japan. Ming officials attempted to enforce neo-Confucian tributary trade principles (codified in the *Ming shilu*, a kind of constitution) in the face of growing maritime trade opportunities and the increasing availability of silver. Crackdowns on trade outside the tributary system sparked violence, often described by modern scholars as piracy.[3] The Ming state's official Supervisors of Maritime Trade and Shipping had hundreds of "sea bandits" captured and hanged in the late 1540s, and most were neither Japanese nor Portuguese. It appears that imperial policies, whether Asian or European, could incite maritime pillage, especially when clamping down on free traders.

Another interesting case from the South China Seas about a century later regards merchant and regional headman Zheng Zhilong and his son, Zheng Chenggong (known to Europeans as Koxinga). Things had grown much more complex in the century since the early Portuguese trading missions. The Zheng were independent coastal traders caught

2. Anthony Reid, "Violence at Sea: Unpacking 'Piracy' in the Claims of States over Asian Seas," in *Elusive Pirates, Pervasive Smugglers: Violence and Clandestine Trade in the Greater China Seas*, ed. Robert Antony (Hong Kong: Hong Kong University Press, 2010), 15–26.
3. See, for example, James Kai-sing Kung and Chicheng Ma, "Autarky and the Rise and Fall of Piracy in Ming China," *Journal of Economic History* 74:2 (June 2014): 509–34; and for context, see Ng Chin-keong, *Boundaries and Beyond: China's Maritime Southeast in Late Imperial Times* (Singapore: NUS Press, 2017), 101–46.

between no less than *five* empires: the collapsing Ming, the rising Qing, the interloping Dutch, the struggling Portuguese, and the silver-rich Spaniards. As the Ming state collapsed in the early 1640s and the Dutch attacked the Spanish and Portuguese (who were also fighting among themselves), the Zheng clan blended trading and raiding to develop a maritime principality anchored to Taiwan. It was only in 1683 that the Qing state thwarted the ambitions of the "pirate king" Koxinga.

Whether in the Adriatic or South China Sea, pirates challenged the claims of princes, mercantile associations, city-states, and even empires, often seeking haven along rugged coasts and among island chains near major shipping lanes. Although they probably bristled at the outlaw label "pirate," many of these seafaring raiders learned to gauge their attacks carefully, so as to profit without drawing deadly reprisals. With time, many such raiders, like the Uskoks of the Adriatic and the Malabaris of southwest India, were drawn into alliances with land-based states and empires wishing to challenge powerful rivals—in this case Venice and the Portuguese—indirectly.

Broader Horizons

The transatlantic voyages of Christopher Columbus beginning in 1492 marked a global turning point, launching a new era in the history of piracy. Even so, Columbus and the subsequent conquest of the Americas must be understood within the framework of Portuguese maritime expansion to the shores of Africa, then Asia. Decades before Columbus, Portuguese slavers and gold traders turned Africa's west coast into a new theater of violent pillage as well as peaceful trade. Some of the first sub-Saharan Africans taken to Europe by sea were captured in what amounted to unprovoked, piratical raids. East Atlantic islands such as the Canaries, Azores, and Cape Verdes became bases for pillage as well as targets for emerging classes of seaborne raiders. As a result, pirate bases also sprang up along the Atlantic coast of Morocco.

By the time of Christopher Columbus' four famous voyages to the Americas, the East Atlantic was a favored hunting ground for French raiders, and they soon moved on to the Caribbean. It was not long before the English, Dutch, and other maritime interlopers resentful of Spain or Portugal ranged not only among Iberia's many claims in the Atlantic but also worldwide. Envious of Iberian success in its violent overseas endeavors, these new raiders sought to take advantage of rich Spanish and Portuguese cargoes of silk fabrics, spices, gold and silver, diamonds, emeralds, pearls, and so on. Spanish and Portuguese vessels and port towns were these pirates' favorite and longest-lasting targets—still plundered in the late eighteenth century. The Spanish *peso de a ocho reales* or silver "piece of eight" became the standard world currency by 1600 or so and thus a favorite pirate objective as well.

Pirates also benefited from new developments in gun manufacture, as well as from innovations in shipbuilding and navigation. Whereas Iberian treasure ships got heavy and defensive in the course of the sixteenth and seventeenth centuries, pirate vessels got increasingly fast and light. Pirates knew how to avoid broadside cannon fire and to make use of smaller weapons. Often expert sailors more at home at sea than on land, pirates customized their vessels and squeezed vital information from captives to learn about currents, shipping itineraries, and port security. In huge open spaces such as the Atlantic basin, this information was vital not only for raiding but also for survival. At their worst, pirates made fatal mistakes due to greed, division, drunkenness, or sheer stupidity—as the castaway Alexander Selkirk, model for Robinson Crusoe, would admit—but at their best they demonstrated extraordinary military prowess and boldness, and some, like Francis Drake, stretched the limits of early modern exploration.

In terms of business models, most pirates organized themselves along joint-stock company lines, pooling resources and sharing out booty according to pre-arranged rules. Many pirates forged alliances with local governors or other royal authorities in exchange for safe haven and access to supplies. This meant giving these sponsors a portion of any booty taken. Escape from the pirate life could be difficult, but some raiders sought pardons for their pillaging by presenting a monarch or prince with maps or other intelligence gathered during the course of a raid. Truly freelance pirates remained rare in the early modern era, as rival empires sought to crush or co-opt them. The overwhelming majority of sea raiders were entangled in one way or another with inter-imperial rivalries.

For a variety of reasons, global piracy peaked between about 1520 and 1720. This was as true in the Caribbean as it was in the Sea of Japan. Piracy did not end for good, but it was greatly diminished. In part, its energies were absorbed by formal naval warfare. As in the case of Rome and the *Mare Nostrum*, random sea raiding faded only when powerful navies were organized to enact widespread suppression campaigns. The memorable case of Captain William Kidd, a pirate hunter turned pirate in the late seventeenth century, shows that these anti-piracy campaigns were sometimes accompanied by treaties and court cases that targeted alleged pirates as rogue subjects whose deeds would no longer be tolerated.[4] Pirates such as Kidd were both products and victims of a mercantilist phase of global commerce.

Thus, global piracy's roughly two hundred year run coincided with ambitious overseas colonial ventures, such as those launched by Portugal, Spain, France, the Netherlands, England, and the Ottoman Empire, yet the phenomenon of sea raiding for profit was also shaped by a whole new age of private enterprise. Piracy was always in between: parasitical on states or empires yet spawned by private initiative. At times it was an extension of other moneymaking ventures. As in the case of Francis Drake, individuals and families formed companies to seek out wealth in trade, planting, mining, livestock raising, and plunder. Though given euphemistic names like "corsairing" or "privateering," piracy was often part of an early modern investment portfolio. Some invested heavily in the slave trade, others in the spice or sugar trades. All found themselves affected by seaborne marauders labeled "pirates," even if they did not openly join them.

As this collection of primary sources from piracy's great age seeks to demonstrate, the various colonial enterprises that made maximum use of new and old sea routes—including those of the Ottomans and Portuguese in the Indian Ocean—gave rise to a new breed of parasite: the global pirate. Put another way, a swift rise in the seaborne movement of precious metals and luxury goods, and more frequent transport of persons rich enough to ransom themselves in cash, proved irresistible for a certain class of predators. Rival empires spent two centuries in the chase before finally developing a lasting means of pirate suppression. But this was the perspective of piracy's victims. For the early modern pirates themselves, the trick was to pull off a great heist somewhere on the far side of the world and live to tell the tale.

---

4. Robert C. Ritchie, *Captain Kidd and the War against the Pirates* (Cambridge, MA: Harvard University Press, 1986), 152–55.

Approaches to Pirate History

Historians have long been drawn to piracy, an inherently dramatic and colorful topic, yet only in the last century or so have scholars attempted to categorize piratical acts according to various models or themes. The historian Philip Gosse spoke of "piracy cycles" in the 1920s, noting that outbreaks or waves of piracy tended to line up with other sequences of events, such as the aftermath of a war.[5] Out-of-work sailors and soldiers were sometimes difficult to control, especially when they followed each other's orders and organized around an objective.

The economist John L. Anderson argued that pirates may be generally categorized as episodic, parasitic, or intrinsic. Episodic pirates were of the kind described by Gosse: seafaring men drawn to a momentary opportunity, only to "fall out" as thieves typically do after spoils were shared or defenses were improved. Parasitic pirates for Anderson constituted a steady but less noticeable phenomenon in the historical record.[6] Parasitic pirates might be fishermen who took advantage of straggling vessels from time to time or traders who picked on any weak vessel that hove into view. More worrisome for some maritime empires were intrinsic pirates, or whole cultures devoted to sea raiding. Rome faced the Cilicians of Anatolia and early modern Venice faced the Uskoks of Dalmatia. The Portuguese felt the same about the Malabaris of southwest India, as did the Spanish with regard to the Caribs of the Windward Islands.

Most historians of the early modern maritime world have shied away from static models or categories in favor of themes tied to long-term change over time. These change-related themes have included (1) the relationship between sea raiding and the rise of international law; (2) crime and corruption as aspects or side effects of the emergence of global capitalism; (3) class formation in relation to maritime trade; and (4) piracy as an extension of imperial competition. Historians of gender and sexuality who have focused on pirates have mostly emphasized continuity by describing the hyper-masculine nature of early modern seaborne life as well as uncovering evidence of homosexual practices among pirate bands. The overwhelmingly male record that piracy left behind makes

---

5. Philip Gosse, *The History of Piracy* (London: Longmans, 1923), 1.
6. John L. Anderson, "Piracy and World History: An Economic Perspective on Maritime Predation," *Journal of World History* 6:2 (Fall 1995): 175–99.

the few documented exceptions of women aboard pirate ships—or those found fighting against them—all the more interesting.

Legal historians have mostly pondered questions of overseas jurisdiction and dominion, for example testing the legal claims of Imperial Rome or the Portuguese Estado da Índia when confronting seaborne marauders. On the flipside, as it were, scholars of the Asian maritime world have repeatedly questioned whether Western legal principles were used to excuse acts of piracy by European intruders as well as to label their victims pirates when they might have been acting in self-defense. Like all legal matters, studies of piracy demand multiple perspectives.

Some historians of empire now speak of pirates as an early modern vanguard, a kind of tacitly encouraged paramilitary force intended to disrupt the commercial and colonial projects of rivals. As will be seen in the case of Henry Morgan, the question of officially sponsored sea raiding comes up constantly in this context. Other historians have linked the rise of Atlantic piracy to the global development of merchant shipping and the creation of a maritime working class. Disgruntled sailors swelled in numbers as the Atlantic, in particular, became more heavily trafficked. Scholars of the slave trade are similarly discovering the significance of piracy in the rise and fall of this nefarious business. Pirates interacted frequently with enslaved Africans, native Americans, and indentured servants of many ethnicities. Ethnohistorians have worked hard to demonstrate the ambivalence typical of pirate interactions with native groups in various parts of the world, testing Eurocentric assumptions and leading scholarship into new and uncharted waters.

To these several approaches to the history of piracy, we would add another means of sorting or categorizing piratical acts based on what the pirates themselves claimed were their principal motives. Certainly pirates were always out for personal gain even if they did not admit it, but typically they gave the following pretexts for their raids: (1) survival; (2) revenge; (3) ethnic or national rivalry; (4) religious or confessional difference; (5) class resentment; and (6) cultural imperatives.

Documented pirate attacks include many instances of raiding for provisions and even water, a reminder that life at sea was difficult in an age before modern food and beverage packaging. Those seafarers not starving might well be stricken with scurvy or suffer a wound or infection, and thus some pirates kidnapped doctors and stole medical supplies. Several pirates claimed personal animus against a government official, an ungenerous prince, or some other malicious individual. Others saw themselves as locked in perpetual war with national or confessional enemies, as in the case of Protestants and Catholics in the sixteenth and seventeenth centuries.

In the Mediterranean, Muslims, Jews, and Christians used religious differences as pretexts for all manner of violent acts, yet just as often they formed convenient alliances in the name of profit. Asian and African waters were, in this sense, infinitely more diverse. According to the historian Marcus Rediker, class resentment among pirates appears most clearly in the eighteenth century, but earlier mutinies and pirate raids were sometimes motivated by short rations and harsh treatment of common sailors.[7] Witness testimonies suggest that Dutch captains could be exceedingly stingy. Finally, some piratical groups, especially those Anderson might term intrinsic pirates, sent young men out to raid and prove their manhood as rites of passage. It is these "intrinsic" pirate cultures that we know least about, as so few produced written sources.

Terminology

Even though contemporaries, particularly victims of seaborne attacks, and modern authors frequently use the term "pirate," in reality not all maritime predators were pirates. Piracy is defined nowadays as the indiscriminate and arbitrary seizure of vessels, goods, and persons at sea.[8] In other words, piracy is robbery, and robbers are criminals. However, since maritime predators operated in disputed waters on the high seas, classifying violent acts as piracy or not often depended on one's perspective.

A term commonly used by Europeans in the sixteenth and seventeenth centuries was "corsair," which implied some level of sponsorship by a sovereign or loyalty to a land-based authority. In this sense, piracy was war by informal means. Beginning in the late Middle Ages, seafaring nations or principalities engaged in armed conflicts licensed private

---

7. Marcus Rediker, *Villains of All Nations: Atlantic Pirates in the Golden Age* (Boston: Beacon, 2004), 19–37, and Rediker, *Between the Devil and the Deep Blue Sea: Merchant Seamen, Pirates, and the Anglo-American Maritime World, 1700–1750* (New York: Cambridge University Press, 1987), 205–53.

8. This broad definition emerges from a number of publications, but confusion persists. For disambiguation, see N.A.M. Rodger, "The Law and Language of Private Naval Warfare," *Mariner's Mirror* 100:1 (Feb. 2014): 5–16.

vessels to supplement their sea power. If successful, largely self-financed corsairs not only weakened the economic base of the enemy but also acquired valuable resources to augment defenses.

In the age of overseas expansion, the concept of licensed maritime raiders soon moved with the conquerors and adventurers across the Atlantic and into the Indian Ocean to become part of the ensuing inter-imperial conflicts all over the globe. Some colonies, such as English Jamaica in its early years, heavily relied on auxiliary forces for defense and economic purposes. By 1661 the term "privateer" emerged for these informal forces, which the English, Dutch, French, and even the Spanish and Portuguese eventually deployed against each other, primarily in wartime. As will be seen in many instances below, ordinary people took to outfitting vessels and going after other ordinary people. Was war, then, not just a thin pretext for continued piracy?

Between illegal piracy and formally authorized privateering was a grey zone. Many raiders who seized prizes, usually vessels flying the wrong flag, tried to find a cover to legalize plunder with dubious commissions, so-called "letters of marque" or "letters of reprisal." Others held valid commissions but failed to declare their prizes after a successful raid, as required by law. Authors use the loosely defined terms "freebooters" and "marauders" for these men.

In the seventeenth-century Caribbean the infamous buccaneers emerged. The name "buccaneer" derives from *boucan*, a Tupi-Guaraní term for a wooden grill, appropriated by French frontiersmen who had spent time in Brazil. The buccaneers as we know them began as hunters in remote parts of Hispaniola and later many turned to raiding and other opportunistic activities directed against the Spaniards. These were often multinational bands, seeking legal prizes but in reality caring little about their victims. From the 1660s until the 1680s, buccaneers served the markets of fledgling non-Spanish colonial economies where few questions were asked if a profit was to be made. Windfalls could be huge, but the number of successful freebooters who managed to escape as rich men and retire in wealth and prosperity was small. In fact, truly successful pirates did not leave a paper trail; therefore, we historians don't even know their names.

All of this suggests that much early modern piracy was in the eye of the beholder. Perpetrators, victims, and sponsors all disagreed on what to call maritime pillage and its principals. It is hoped that this collection of sources will encourage readers to ponder the variable uses of the above terms (pirate, corsair, buccaneer, privateer, freebooter, marauder), and thus to explore the ambiguities of early modern sea raiding. What legal language was used to criminalize certain forms of maritime raiding, and what did sea bandits do to legitimize or justify robbery and other serious crimes? How did shifts in official discourse and diplomacy affect attempts at reprisal or suppression? These and other questions hint at the complexity of the subject matter.

Pirates in the Archives

Without seeking to strip the pirates of mystery, this collection of primary documents aims to introduce students directly to a wide variety of seaborne marauders at a time when European maritime powers, as well as the Ottomans, Qing, and several other non-Christian principalities and empires, were engaged in overseas expansion. Imperial consolidation in South and East Asia was of central importance to pirate activities even when overseas expansion was not the main aim. The pirates' enemies and victims are also represented. Furthermore, we have selected a blend of published and unpublished manuscript sources—several taken directly from the archives and translated here for the first time—to provide rare insight into the actions of famous as well as unnamed robbers.

The sources mostly fall under the following types: (1) legal opinions; (2) travelers' memoirs; (3) official letters and reports; (4) inventories; (5) witness or victim testimonies; (6) pacts or agreements; (7) confessions; (8) sermons; and (9) poems.

Historians continue to unearth new written records of piratical activity in the archives, and maritime archaeologists have added material evidence in recent years. In this volume we have sought to introduce readers to some newly discovered, non-English manuscript sources in translation in hopes of encouraging further research and deeper questioning of well-known, often printed sources. Learning to place fragmentary archival evidence in context and interpreting it in terms of its time rather than ours are constant challenges in the field of history—all the more so when dealing with groups that were maligned by many of their contemporaries.

We remind readers that all sources are biased in that they represent a point of view or an argument, and several of the sources reproduced in this volume were not written up immediately after the events described.

The written evidence of piracy is like many things in history, riddled with gaps and silences. We have undertaken every effort to insert the voices of women and non-Europeans, but the overwhelming majority of surviving sources were composed by western European male subjects. However, if these records are placed in a historical context and read with care, a picture with many different facets emerges. Occasionally, one discovers unexpected voices hidden inside "traditional" sources.

SECTION I: GLOBAL PIRACY AND EUROPEAN LAW

> For a pirate is not included in the list of lawful enemies, but is the common enemy of all.[1]—Cicero

Christopher Columbus' early voyages to the Caribbean prompted Spain and Portugal to legalize their overseas claims. Pope Alexander VI, who happened to be Spanish, issued a bull, or decree, in 1493 known as *Inter Caetera* that led to the 1494 Treaty of Tordesillas. Though sometimes derided as an attempt to divide the world's oceans into two equal halves, *Inter Caetera* was a grant of dominion over "newly discovered" lands, islands, and their inhabitants in exchange for spreading Roman Catholicism. In practice, Spain and Portugal found that keeping interlopers away from their lands and subjects overlapped with policing the seas. The Iberians faced many challengers, but it was the Dutch who first justified their actions by law. As described below, jurist Hugo Grotius led the charge. In the first decades of the seventeenth century he argued for an open system, what has come to be known as the principle of the "freedom of the seas." Notably, it was the English who responded with a different legal argument, more in line with older Roman notions of sea suzerainty, or the Ciceronian principle of *Mare Clausum*. All of these legal arguments, batted back and forth between early modern seafaring empires, came to define piracy as a global maritime menace in need of suppression. By the turn of the eighteenth century, the emerging British Empire took up the burden of global antipiracy enforcement, backed by a sheaf of royal decrees.

---

1. Cicero, *De Officiis*, book 3, ch. 29, 107.

1

DOCUMENT 1

Dutch Counterpoint: The Legal Opinion of Hugo Grotius (c.1603–1604)[2]

In response to the sweeping colonial claims of Spain and Portugal, Dutch jurist Hugo Grotius proposed an open sea model. Grotius' concept of the "freedom of the seas," much like the ancient notion of pirates as "enemies of human kind," became a pillar of international law. Grotius laid out the legal principle of the "freedom of the seas" in his widely quoted treatise, Mare Liberum *(1609). Yet scholars have pointed to the significance of Grotius' initial defense of Dutch despoliation of Portuguese merchants in Southeast Asian waters, specifically a Dutch attack on the carrack* Santa Catarina *in 1603 near Singapore. Known later as* De Indis *("On the Indies"), Grotius' tract was initially called* De Jurae Praedae, *or "On the Law of Prize and Booty." Its aim was to justify violent plunder of a non-military vessel by a Dutch subject not acting on official orders.*

De Jurae Praedae, Chapter IV, Question II, Article I: Is the seizure of prize or booty ever just?

In the first place, with reference to those cases in which we take up arms for the purpose of recovering our own property, there is no question but that we may rightly employ military force to divert unjust possession from an armed possessor. For who can fail to perceive that, when we are granted the right to acquire for ourselves those things which are useful, the further right to guard such things after they have been acquired and to recover them if they are taken from us, is implicitly conceded at the same time? But if I am not able to regain the actual piece of property involved, then that unjust possessor is nevertheless my debtor to the extent of the value of the said property. Therefore, I should be permitted to obtain from among his goods the equivalent of his debt to me.... Nature herself ... grants me the permission to acquire in any way whatsoever, from him through whom I suffer the loss of property belonging to

---

2. Source: Hugo Grotius, *Commentary on the Law of Prize and Booty* [1603], intr. Martine Julia van Ittersum (Indianapolis: Liberty Fund, 2006), 73–74.

me, the exact equivalent of that lost property, and the thing so acquired becomes my own.

DOCUMENT 2

Death to All Pirates: The Legal Opinion of Leoline Jenkins (c.1668)[3]

It was near the end of Queen Elizabeth I's long reign from 1558 to 1603 that the English jurist Sir Edward Coke defined the pirate as a felonious sea robber who was something worse: hostis humani generis, *"the enemy of all human kind." In Coke's opinion, drawing from classical Western authorities, robbing people on the open sea, already a treacherous and even deadly space, was categorically worse than doing so on land. The distinction was important, and although this was an English legal opinion, it would have global repercussions that persist in international law. Sir Leoline Jenkins was a Welsh jurist who served on England's Admiralty (or maritime affairs) Court between 1665 and 1673. Building on Coke's opinions, Jenkins made some further distinctions about piracy, noting that the offense must be by definition armed and violent, causing fear or terror. As such it was to be defined as a capital crime. Jenkins also considered the matter of English subjects as pirates against foreign nations, already raised by Coke.*

Charge to the Jury, c.1668

There are some sorts of felonies and offenses, which cannot be committed anywhere else but upon the sea, within the jurisdiction of the Admiralty. These I shall insist upon a little more particularly, and the chiefest of this kind is piracy.

---

3. Source: William Wynne, *The Life of Sir Leoline Jenkins, Judge of the High-Court of Admiralty.* 2 vols. (London: Joseph Downing, 1724), vol. 1, 86. (Available online but also re-published in James Brown Scott, ed., *Cases on International Law: Selected from the Decisions of English and American Courts* [Boston: Boston Book Co., 1902], 345.)

You are therefore to inquire of all Pirates and sea-rovers; they are in the eye of the law *hostes humani generis*, enemies not of one nation or one sort of people only, but of all mankind. They are outlawed, as I may say, by the laws of all nations, that is, out of the protection of all princes and of all laws whatsoever. Everybody is commissioned and is to be armed against them, as against rebels and traitors, to subdue and to root them out.

That which is called robbing upon the highway, the same thing being done upon the water is called piracy. Now robbery, as 'tis distinguished from thieving or larceny, implies not only the actual taking away of my goods, while I am, as we say, in peace, but also the putting me in fear, by taking them away by force and arms out of my hands, or in my sight and presence; when this is done upon the sea, without lawful commission of war or reprisals, it is downright piracy.

And such was the generosity of our ancient English, such the abhorrence of our laws against pirates and sea-rovers, that if any of the King's subjects robbed or murdered a foreigner upon our seas or within our ports, though the foreigner happened to be of a nation in hostility against the King, yet, if he had the King's passport, or the Lord Admiral's, the offender was published, not as a felon only, but this crime was made high treason, in that the great Prince Henry the Fifth's time; and not only himself, but all his accomplices were to suffer as traitors against the crown and dignity of the King.

DOCUMENT 3

The High Court of Admiralty Defines Piracy (1696)[4]

Despite shrill decrees, global piracy flourished in the later seventeenth century. English subjects in particular ran amok, not only despoiling the Spanish and Portuguese but also the Mughals and other Asian princes. When pirates such as Henry Avery pillaged ships belonging to these and other East India Company allies, the government in London came under enormous pressure to

---

4. Source: *The Tryals of Joseph Dawson, Edward Forseith, William May, William Bishop, James Lewis, and John Sparkes for several Robberies* (London: John Everingham, 1696), 6.

take action. One measure was to bring Avery and his men to trial. However, the captain vanished and could not be apprehended. Thus the trial of six crewmembers captured in Ireland was meant to send a reassuring message to the Mughals. In October 1696 the men had to stand trial for the assault on Indian vessels, but the jury acquitted all defendants. Not spared by double jeopardy, within a few days a new trial was set up in which the six were charged with having committed piracy under a different set of circumstances. At the beginning of the court proceedings Judge Sir Charles Hedges outlined the legal framework for the jury.

Sir Charles Hedges to Grand Jury, 31 October 1696

Now piracy is only a sea term for robbery, piracy being a robbery committed within the jurisdiction of the Admiralty. If any man be affected within that jurisdiction and his ship or goods violently taken away without a legal authority, this is robbery and piracy. If the mariners of any ship shall violently dispossess the master and afterwards carry away the ship itself, or any of the goods, or tackle, apparel or furniture, with a felonious intention, in any place where the Lord Admiral has or pretends to have jurisdiction, this is also robbery and piracy. The intention will, in these cases, appear by considering the end for which the fact was committed and the end will be known, if the evidence shall show you what has been done.

Now the jurisdiction of the Admiralty is declared, and described in the statute [28 Hen 8, c. 15], and commission by virtue of which we here meet, and is extended throughout all seas, and the ports, havens, creeks and rivers beneath the first bridge next the sea, even under the higher watermark.

The King of England has not only an empire and sovereignty over the British seas, but also an undoubted jurisdiction and power in concurrency with other princes and states for the punishment of all piracies and robberies at sea in the most remote parts of the world so that if any person whatsoever, native or foreigner, Christian of infidel, Turk or pagan, with whose country we have no war with whom we hold trade and correspondence and are in amity shall be robbed or spoiled in the narrow seas, the Mediterranean, Atlantic, Southern, or any other seas, or the branches thereof, either on this or the other side of the line, it is piracy within the limits of your enquiry and the cognizance of the court.

DOCUMENT 4

The Weak Arm of the Law (1717)[5]

English subjects proved to be an enduring menace abroad. In 1716 and early 1717 the British government received a torrent of complaints from colonial authorites about assaults of Jamaican raiders who initially looted a shipwrecked Spanish treasure fleet on the east coast of Florida and then expanded their predatory activities to other parts of the Atlantic. Most of these beachcombers-turned-pirates were based in the sparsely populated Bahamas, from where they increasingly assaulted British merchant shipping. Since the Royal Navy was not prepared to police American waters, the government decided to dispatch Woodes Rogers, a loyal privateer and former circumnavigator, to the Bahamas. Knowing that Rogers' forces were too weak to chase down all raiders, the crown offered amnesty to all pirates who surrendered to colonial officials. It turned out, however, that many pirates accepted the amnesty as a kind of life insurance and soon reverted to their old habits.

By the King,
A Proclamation for Suppressing of Pirates

George R.

Whereas we have received information that several persons, subjects of Great Britain, since the 24th day of June, in the year of our Lord 1715, committed divers piracies and robberies upon the high seas in the West Indies, or adjoining to our plantations, which has, and may occasion great damage to the merchants of Great Britain, and others, trading into those parts. And though we have appointed such a force as we judge

---

5. Source: The National Archives, Privy Council 2/86, fol. 21. (Published in *The London Gazette*, September 17, 1717.)

sufficient for suppressing the said piracies: Yet the more effectually to put an end to the same, we have thought fit, by and with the advice of our Privy Council, to issue this our Royal Proclamation; and we do hereby promise and declare that in case any of the said pirates shall, on or before the 5th day of September, in the year of our Lord 1718 surrender him or themselves to one of our principal secretaries of state in Great Britain or Ireland, or to any governor or deputy-governor of any of our plantations or dominions beyond the seas, every such pirate and pirates, so surrendering him or themselves, as aforesaid, shall have our gracious pardon of and for such his or their piracy or piracies, by him or them committed before the 5th day of January next ensuing. And we do hereby strictly charge and command all our admirals, captains and other officers at sea, and all our governors and commanders of any forts, castles or other places in our plantations and all other our officers, civil and military, to seize and take such of the pirates who shall refuse or neglect to surrender themselves accordingly. And we do hereby further declare that in case any person or persons, on or after the 6th day of September 1718 shall discover or seize, or cause or procure to be discovered or seized, any one or more of the said pirates, so neglecting or refusing to surrender themselves, as aforesaid, so as they may be brought to justice, and convicted of the said offense, such person or persons, so making such discovery or seizure, or causing or procuring such discovery or seizure to be made, shall have and receive as a reward for the same, viz. for every commander of any pirate ship or vessel the sum of 100 pounds; for every lieutenant, master, boatswain, carpenter, and gunner, the sum of 40 pounds; for every inferior officer the sum of 30 pounds; and for every private man the sum of 20 pounds. And if any person or persons, belonging to, and being part of the crew of any such pirate ship or vessel, shall, on or after the said 6th day of September 1718 seize and deliver, or cause to be seized or delivered, any commander or commanders of such pirate ship or vessel so as that he or they be brought to justice and convicted of the said offense, such person or persons, as a reward for the same, shall receive for every such commander the sum of 200 pounds; which said sums the Lord Treasurer, or the commissioners of our Treasury for the time being, are hereby required and directed to pay accordingly.

Given at Our Court at Hampton Court, the 5th Day of September 1717, in the Fourth Year of Our Reign.

God Save the King

Questions to consider for Section I:

How did early modern legal scholars distinguish pirates from land-based robbers?

How did the English and the Dutch treat despoliation of foreign vessels differently?

How did anti-piracy laws set the stage for international maritime cooperation, and why?

What leverage did early modern sea raiders have in the face of legal suppression?

SECTION II: ATLANTIC EXPANSION AND THE FIRST GLOBAL PIRATES

After 1500 Atlantic sea-lanes filled seasonally with slow-sailing Spanish and Portuguese vessels loaded with Asian spices, American precious metals, and even African slaves. These were too enticing to pass up for French, English, Dutch, and Moroccan corsairs, especially when war with Spain or Portugal offered a pretext. Iberian claims in Asia drew similar reactions from sea-raiding peoples, among them the Malabaris of India and the so-called dwarf pirates of Japan and China. The following document selections offer a sense of Iberian but also general maritime vulnerability in the sixteenth century, when no sovereign could make much of a claim except at the point of a gun.

DOCUMENT 5

Piracy in the Portuguese Atlantic (c.1548)[1]

The German gunner and mercenary Hans Staden sailed across the Atlantic, participating in the early Portuguese colonization of Brazil. Staden is famous for his memoir of life as a captive among the Tupi speakers of Brazil's south coast, but he also found himself in a number of piratical scrapes, including one off the Azores, a chain of mid-Atlantic islands used by the Portuguese to refit and supply ships coming back from India, Africa, and the Americas. According to Staden, early Atlantic pirates saw the Azores as an ideal hunting ground. Staden published an account of his Atlantic adventures upon returning to Germany in 1557 as a testimonial of divine deliverance. Staden leaves us to ask: Was he a pirate, too?

---

1. Source: Hans Staden, *Hans Staden's True History: An Account of Cannibal Captivity in Brazil* [1557], ed. and trans. Neil L. Whitehead and Michael Harbsmeier (Durham: Duke University Press, 2008), 29–30.

We sailed for 40 miles . . . to a harbor called Paraíba, Brazil, where we meant to load a cargo of brazil wood and to raid the natives for more provisions. As we arrived there, we found a ship from France that was loading wood, and we attacked it, hoping to capture it. However, they destroyed our mainmast with one shot and sailed away; several on our ship were killed or wounded.

We then decided to set out once more for Portugal, for due to contrary winds we could not return to the harbor, where we had intended to get provisions. With unfavorable winds and very sparse supplies, we sailed to Portugal, suffering greatly from hunger; some ate the goatskins that we had on board. Each day they gave each of us a small scoop of water and a little manioc flour. We were 108 days at sea. On the 12th of August we arrived at the islands called the Azores that belong to the king of Portugal. There we anchored, rested, and fished. Here we saw a ship at sea, and sailed toward it to see what manner of ship it was. It was a pirate who defended himself, but we gained the upper hand and captured the ship. The pirates escaped in the boats, sailing toward the islands. The ship contained lots of wine and bread, which refreshed us.

After this, we encountered five ships belonging to the king of Portugal. They were awaiting the ships from India, to escort them to Portugal. We remained with them, and helped to escort a ship arriving from India to the island of Terceira, where we remained. A lot of ships, all of which had come from the New World, had assembled at the island, some bound for Spain, some for Portugal. We left Terceira in the company of almost a hundred ships, and arrived in Lisbon about the 8th of October, in the year 1548. We had been voyaging for sixteen months.

DOCUMENT 6

Casual Piracy in the North Atlantic (c.1556)[2]

Jean de Léry was a Protestant minister sent to the failed colony of "Antarctic France," in Brazil's Guanabara Bay, about the time

---

2. Source: Jean de Léry, *History of a Voyage to the Land of Brazil* [1578], ed. and trans. Janet Whatley (Berkeley: University of California Press, 1990), 8–9.

Hans Staden was writing up his memoirs in Germany. Like Staden, Léry is best known for writing about life among Tupi-speaking Brazilians, but he also experienced piracy on the high seas. In this case, the French colonists ran into trouble—or opportunity— while heading into the open Atlantic from the English Channel, destination Brazil. As in Staden's case, the "law of the strong" seemed to prevail. Also like Staden, Léry framed his story in terms of divine providence.

We were, then, tossed about, and we navigated with great difficulty until the thirteenth day after our embarkation, when God pacified the swell and storms of the sea. The following Sunday we met two English merchant ships that were coming from Spain. When our sailors accosted them, and saw that there was much to be had aboard, they nearly pillaged them. And indeed, as I have said, our three vessels were well furnished with artillery and other munitions; our sailors therefore were overbearing and arrogant, and when weaker vessels found themselves at their mercy they were by no means safe.

I must say here, since it has come up in connection with this first encounter with a ship, that I have seen practiced on the sea what is also done most often on land: that is, he who has weapons in his fist, and who is the strongest, carries the day, and imposes the law on his companion. The way it goes for these mariner gentlemen, striking sail, and meeting with the poor merchant ships, usually claim that they have been unable to approach any land or port because of tempests and calms, and that they are consequently short of supplies, for which they are willing to pay. But if, under this pretext, they can set foot on board their neighbor's ship, you need hardly ask whether, as an alternative to scuttling the vessel, they relieve it of whatever takes their fancy. And if one then protests (as in fact we always did) that no order has been given to pillage indiscriminately, friends as well as enemies, they give you the common cant of our land soldiers, who in such cases offer as sole reason that it's war and custom, and that you have to get used to it.

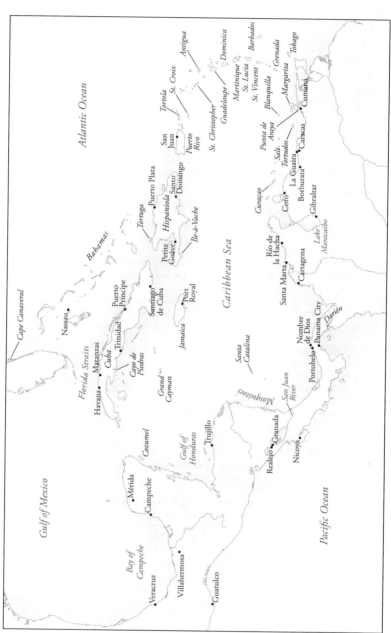

Map of the Caribbean showing the hunting grounds of the pirates.

DOCUMENT 7 (IN FOUR PARTS)

John Hawkins of Plymouth, Slaver and Corsair along the Spanish Main (1565–1568)[3]

In the 1560s several families from England's West Country began to organize slaving and trading voyages to the Spanish Caribbean by way of West Africa. These voyages, sanctioned by Queen Elizabeth I, aimed to break Philip II of Spain's claims of monopoly control of the Caribbean and to break Portugal's claims on Africa. The English slavers' leader, John Hawkins of Plymouth, alternated between pleas and threats as he attempted to sell slaves—many of them kidnapped from their villages in Africa—to Caribbean colonists who feared retaliation from their own government. The following series of documents relate to Hawkins' early voyages to mainland South America—today the Caribbean coast of Venezuela and Colombia—in 1565 and 1568. By comparing perspectives, one may see how various Spanish officials responded to Hawkins' offers and threats, and how he interpreted their responses. Hawkins made a common claim used by contraband traders: he had been blown ashore in Spanish America due to contrary winds. A common European custom was to allow foreign ships in need to refit and take on supplies when such unexpected events occurred. It is important to note that, in the 1560s, England and Spain were not at war.

Part 1. Antonio de Barros to Licenciate Alonso Bernáldez, governor of Borburata, Venezuela, April 4, 1565

Very Magnificent Sir:

The clumsiness of my pen and brevity of the time available have constrained me to write by the hand of another. The situation is that yesterday, Tuesday, there appeared off this town seven sails, one of which vessels is very powerful. The fleet is English and so rich in slaves and merchandise that they affirm it to be worth more than 100,000 pesos. The commander is an Englishman who time past came to Santo Domingo.

---

3. Source: Irene A. Wright, *Spanish Documents Concerning English Voyages to the Caribbean, 1527–1568* (London: Hakluyt Society, 1929), 76–77, 82–83, 107–8, 116–19.

He advertises that he is a great servitor of his majesty [Philip II]. His intention is to sell with authorization and unless this license is given him he threatens with great oaths to do what harm and damage he may be able.

Your honor is already aware of the necessity existing in all the province and of the serious illnesses all the province is suffering because of its penury. I entreat your honor to deign to come to apply the remedy, for the best good of all. All the settlements will ask and formally demand it and even furnish depositions as to the general need and hardship and epidemics due to this situation, in which matter neither God, Our Lord, nor his majesty is well served. The royal revenues would be augmented and the country benefitted, for this captain promises to please everybody. He brings more than 400 negroes.

If by chance your honor does not come to apply the remedy, as we all desire and entreat your honor to do, having taken the measures above said, of having all the people ask it and furnish depositions, I beg your honor to deign to extend the license and open up the way, for in addition to the benefit and relief this would mean to all, and increase of the royal revenue, to do so will obviate the great damage and hardship we anticipate.

The captain has agreed to wait ten days, to be reckoned from tomorrow, Thursday the 5th, and so it behoves your honor to hurry or at least send some messenger to advise of your honor's arrival, for which we confidently hope, since it would be an act of great charity and relief to all.

What gold there was in his majesty's chest, [Juan] Pacheco carries. I see no better remedy than to let this fellow sell, for in addition to the duties he will pay, a quantity of gold will be smelted . . .

There is nothing more to write except to entreat you honor to come. Greater evil is ahead of us, for if the town is burned it will mean its abandonment, in addition to which we will be turned into the woods in weather bad enough to kill us even were we strong, as we are not, but very sickly.

Our Lord preserve the magnificent person of your honor, augmenting your honor's estate with higher offices in his holy service.

There is no news of any sort except that the writer kisses your honor's hands and begs to remain yours,

From Borburata, 4 April 1565

Very magnificent sir, your servant kisses your honor's hands,

Antonio de Barros

Part 2. John Hawkins to Licenciate Alonso Bernáldez, April 16, 1565

On the 16th day of April in the year 1565 the following petition was presented before the governor, Licenciate Bernáldez:

Very magnificent sir: I, John Hawkins, captain general of my fleet, in the person of Cristobal de Llerena, my procurator, appear before your honor in the manner most advantageous to my interests, and state that:

Whereas by order of Elizabeth, queen of England, my mistress, whose fleet this is, I cleared on a certain voyage and was by contrary weather driven to these coasts where, since I have found a convenient harbor it behoves me to repair and refurnish my ships to continue said voyage.

And whereas to do this I must sell the slaves and merchandise I carry.

And whereas I am a great servitor of the majesty of King Philip, whom I served when he was king of England.

I therefore petition your honor to grant me license to sell my cargo. I stand ready to pay his majesty the duties usual in this land and to sell the said merchandise at acceptable prices.

And whereas in addition to repairing and refurnishing my fleet I am obliged to pay my ships and men in each port entered.

And whereas I do not desire to offend or occasion difficulties, petitioning, as I petition, your honor to grant me the license requested under which to sell to the Spaniards in order that I may purchase of them.

If this petition be not granted, I shall seek my own solution, for I cannot leave this port, nor will I leave, without supplying my said necessities, for even were I willing to do so, yet am I unable, for I cannot prevail with my people.

Therefore, since between Spain and England there is no enmity nor war, and this fleet belongs to the queen, my mistress, of which and of all else herein stated I am ready to furnish depositions, let your honor not anger me nor move me to aught that I should not do, as will be inevitable if your honor refuse me the license I ask. I protest that if from its refusal harm and damage follow, the fault and responsibility will be your honor's.

I ask for witnesses to this petition and a certificate.

John Hawkins

Part 3. Miguel de Castellanos to the Spanish crown, Río de la Hacha (today Riohacha), Colombia, January 1, 1568

Catholic Royal Majesty

During the time that I have resided in this city as your majesty's treasurer, which is more than fourteen years, it has been continuously beset by French, English, and other corsairs who regularly besiege it; and since this land is without arms and unprovided with necessary materials of war, they frequently endanger its safety.

Especially was this true in the month of May in the year 1567 when Jean Bontemps, commanding ten French ships, came to take this city and sent ashore to demand license to trade, threatening that unless it was extended to him he would burn the place and leave everything desolate. I dissimulated with him for a day, during which I gathered the women and children and invalids into my house, where I furnished them necessary subsistence at my own expense, while I assembled the rest of the people. We went down to meet the corsair, who had disembarked with 200 men and much artillery, and with what little ordnance this place could bring up, we played on them and beat them, so that they ran at full speed and withdrew to their ships, and made sail and fled, and fell upon Santa Marta, which place it is said they took, along with a very good ship of the fleet.

A few days later another large fleet of English galleons and ships appeared, in command of John Lovell, and he made extensive preparations to trade in this town. Seeing that this was not permitted to him, they played many guns upon us, against which we defended ourselves so that we beat them into flight.

After this fashion this city has had many encounters with these corsairs and others, who are so hard put to it that they advertise that they mean to assemble large armadas to capture me and destroy this place. In all this I have exercised the vigilance due to your majesty's royal service, and at my own expense I defend and will continue to defend the city, with all my strength. I thought advisable to inform your majesty of this, that your majesty might know the situation and the intention I entertain in this matter, as in all others, to live and die in the royal service, and for its good to expend what I possess, and also that if it appear that in so important a matter further defense be necessary than that which exists, which assuredly is little, orders may be issued to furnish what your majesty may provide.

Our Lord preserve your majesty's life with increase of many more kingdoms, as we, your majesty's servants, desire.

Río de la Hacha, 1 January 1568

Catholic Royal Majesty, your majesty's least servant kisses your majesty's royal feet.

Miguel de Castellanos

Part 4. Lázaro de Vallejo Aldrete and Hernando Costilla to the Spanish Crown, Río de la Hacha, September 20, 1568

Catholic Royal Majesty

On 10 June last, John Hawkins, English corsair, arrived off this port with ten warships, all well armed and supplied with artillery and fireworks and many other weapons and equipment suitable to so powerful an armada as his. He carried more than 600 men very well armed and outfitted with corselets and arquebuses and pikes and crossbows and halberds and all other weapons that could be carried, suitable to attack. In good order they landed next day about noon, half a league from this city. Their pinnaces and ships played many guns, for which reason Miguel de Castellanos, your majesty's general in command, was unable to prevent them from landing.

He went out to encounter them with as many as 60 men, whom he had succeeded in assembling, and with this, the small force he had, he offered as fine and valorous a defense as has ever been made in these Indies, and killed more than 30 of the enemy. He rendered such signal service that all were astonished at his great valor (both his adversaries and also the residents), for certainly it was a business that today, on looking back at it, fills with fright those who were present and those who hear it related.

In good order he withdrew with his small force without losing a man, whereas truly it seemed incredible that any should have escaped, and the English general took the town. Indignant to discover that your majesty's commander should have undertaken with so few soldiers to prevent him from taking it, and because certain gentlemen whom he much esteemed had been killed, he set fire to the town and burned nearly two-thirds of it and blew up the government house.

This done, he began next day to march inland in very good order, his field [cannon] in advance. Observing this, your majesty's general summoned what force he could and took up a position ahead of him, to prevent his advance in so far as possible, burning what houses were in the country and driving off the livestock, that the enemy might not obtain possession of it. In doing this your majesty's general performed many valorous deeds and killed some of the enemy's men, seeing which the English general determined to return to the town from which point he had arrived, which was more than a league from the city. He retired in the same good order in which he had advanced. His intention was to march again into the interior at night, since he could not accomplish his purpose by day.

He dared to venture this because he had possession of a mulatto and a negro, slaves of your majesty's general, who deserted to and, that he might liberate them, offered to lead him to the place where your majesty's treasure-box was buried and where most of the people of this city were, with their goods.

With this in view they set out at midnight with these guides, and three hours before dawn arrived where your majesty's general had a tent with much property and where the said citizens were with their goods. The enemy captured a married man with his wife and children and other townsfolk and took all the goods and negroes that were there.

The enemy having captured this booty, the city townsfolk and persons whom the Englishman had captured sent one of their number to your majesty's general that he might ransom them and their goods, for the Englishman had told them that unless they were ransomed he would kill them and carry off all that he had taken from them. He repeated this threat often and truly it inspired great pity to see them so afflicted and in such danger.

Seeing this, your majesty's general, moved by his great commiseration for the said townsfolk, resolved to ransom them from the Englishman, that he might not carry out his cruel threat, and so they and all their goods and the houses of the town that remained unburned were ransomed for 4,000 pesos in gold . . .

We entreat your majesty to remedy the grievous conditions prevailing today in the Indies. For every two ships that come hither from Spain, twenty corsairs appear. For this reason not a town on all this coast is safe, for whenever they please to do so they take and plunder these settlements. They go so far as to boast that they are lords of the sea and of the land, and as a matter of fact daily we see them seize ships, but those of the Indies trade and also some that come here from Spain itself. They capture towns, and this so commonly that we see it happen every year. Unless your majesty deign to favor all this coast by remedying the situation, all these settlements must necessarily be abandoned, from which will result grave detriment to your majesty's royal patrimony and an end will be put to the inter-Indies traffic; trade with the Canaries will suffer, as will also those ships that come out of Spain between fleets.

God, Our Lord, preserve the exalted and very powerful person of your majesty and grant your majesty prosperity through many years and increase your majesty's kingdoms and dominions as we, your majesty's loyal servitors, desire.

Río de la Hacha, 26 September 1568

Your royal Catholic majesty's humble servants who kiss your majesty's royal feet,

Lázaro de Vallejo Aldrete, Hernando Castillo

DOCUMENT 8

Francis Drake Attacks Nombre de Dios, Panama (1572)[4]

Francis Drake was a junior cousin of John Hawkins. He participated in several of the early slave trading expeditions to the Caribbean described above, culminating in a shared disaster off the port of Veracruz in 1568. Humiliated by Mexico's arriving viceroy and lucky to escape with his life, Drake vowed to seek revenge by "singeing the king of Spain's beard" despite England's official peace with Spain. Now a declared corsair rather than a simple contraband trader and in the eyes of the Spanish a pirate, Drake set out in the summer of 1572 to capture a pile of Spanish silver and gold warehoused at Nombre de Dios on Panama's north coast as it awaited the royal fleet for transport to Europe. Drake soon discovered that a number of enslaved Africans had managed to run away from the Spanish and establish autonomous communities in the rainforest. Known as cimarrones *in Spanish, the "maroons" or "cimaroons" of Panama became essential helpers of Drake and other Englishmen in these years. The following excerpt was written by an unknown member of the expedition.*

We made our stand in the midst of the market place, where a tree grows very close to the cross. From there our Captain [Drake] sent some of our

---

4. Source: *Francis Drake, Privateer: Contemporary Narratives and Documents,* ed. John Hampden (Tuscaloosa: University of Alabama Press, 1972), 60, 71.

men to stop the ringing of the alarm bell, which had continued all this while. But the church being very strongly built and fast shut, they could not without firing (which our captain forbade) get into the steeple where the bell hung.

In the meantime, our captain having taken two or three Spaniards as they fled, commanded them to show him the governor's house, where he understood was the ordinary place of unloading the mules of all the treasure which came from Panama by the King's appointment, although the silver was only kept there; the gold, pearl, and jewels (being there once entered by the King's officer) was carried from there to the King's treasure house not far off, being a house very strongly built of lime and stone, for the safe keeping thereof.

At our coming to the governor's house we found the great door, where the mules usually unload, even then opened, a candle lighted upon the top of the stairs; and a fair [she-mule] ready saddled, either for the governor himself, or some other of his household to carry it after him. By means of this light we saw a huge heap of silver in that back room; being a pile of bars of silver of, as near as we could guess, 70 foot in length, of 10 foot in breadth, and twelve foot in height, piled up against the wall. Each bar was between 35 and 40 pounds in weight.

[Although the English got close enough to see this enormous stack of Peruvian silver, they were soon driven out of Nombre de Dios, with Drake bleeding heavily from an arquebus shot in the leg. Most of the Englishmen returned to their vessels, but a parley with the Spanish and intelligence from an escaped African slave convinced them not to attempt a new assault on Nombre de Dios. After reconnoitering the coast and restoring some supplies, the English sought the aid of runaway slaves in eastern Panama, the famous *cimarrones* of Ballano. After another parley, the English went ashore:]

The next day [September 14] we arrived at this designated river, where we found the Cimaroons according to promise. The rest of their number were a mile upstream, in a wood by the river's side. There, after we had given them entertainment and received good testimonies of their joy and good will toward us, we took two more of them into our pinnaces, leaving our two men with the rest of theirs to march by land to another river called Rio Guana, intending to meet there with another company of cimaroons which were now in the mountains.

So we departed that day from Rio Diego with our pinnaces toward our ship . . .

DOCUMENT 9 (IN 4 PARTS)

Contrasting Views from Francis Drake's Famous Voyage (1577–1580)[5]

After mixed success raiding in the Spanish Caribbean, Drake organized a more ambitious voyage aimed at pillaging Spanish shipping in the Pacific. The so-called Famous Voyage, which made Drake the first European after Magellan to circumnavigate the globe and which won him a knighthood from Queen Elizabeth I, involved a number of surprise raids along with collection of intelligence—including Spanish pilots—and a search for the fabled Northwest Passage linking the North Atlantic to the North Pacific. First is a description of Spanish ships captured on the coast of Ecuador, 1579, from the second declaration of John Drake, nephew of Francis, in Spanish custody. The first three testimonies are translated from the Spanish. The last is Drake's own report on the seizure of the great silver ship he called the Cacaplata. *Each testimony offers a different perspective on the same sequence of events.*

Part 1. A Spanish narrative of Drake's capture of the ship *Cacaplata*

On arriving at the Cape of San Francisco they found another bark in which some friars were traveling. Drake's men took this also, sending her occupants in the boat to the shore, which was near, but detaining the owner of the bark and his nephew, who was a clerk, and some negroes.

---

5. Source: Zelia Nuttall, *New Light on Drake: A Collection of Documents Relating to His Voyage of Circumnavigation, 1577–1580,* 2nd ser. no. 34 (London: Hakluyt Society, 1914), 48–49, 156–58, 301. The anonymous English account is in *Francis Drake, Privateer: Contemporary Narratives and Documents,* ed. John Hampden (Tuscaloosa: University of Alabama Press, 1972), 170–71.

After seizing the gold that they found on board the clerk said that there was no more but the negroes said there was. Captain Francis ordered that the clerk was to be hanged by the neck to a beam so that he should declare whether there was more gold. The clerk said that there was not and that the negroes had lied.

Not having found more [gold], Captain Francis released the clerk and carried the barque, in tow, until they perceived the vessel of San Juan de Antón, which he espied at a distance of about three leagues. In order to take her, Captain Francis pretended not to follow her and, to prevent his galleon from sailing too fast, he hung out many cables and mattresses which went dragging along. He lowered his sails and hid his pinnace at the off side of his galleon. Toward dusk San Juan de Antón came toward him and they hailed each other. By order of Captain Francis the Spaniards who were in his galleon said "that it was the ship of Miguel Ángel," to which San Juan de Antón responded "that this could not be for he had left that ship empty at Callao." He challenged them to "strike sail in the name of the King." Captain Francis, in turn, challenged them to "strike sail in the name of the Queen of England" and shot a cannon at them which carried off her mizzen [mast]. An arrow shot wounded San Juan de Antón and he struck sail.

So they took the vessel, with much silver and carried her with them for three days until a calm befell them, when they were able to transfer the silver to the galleon of Captain Francis. They then released San Juan de Antón's ship, with her crew and the remainder of her cargo, on the route from Paita, and pursuing their course, they went to the island of Caño. There they anchored and Captain Francis careened his ship, in order to clean her. While there, a barque passed by, coming from Nicaragua and laden with maize and sarsaparilla. This was taken by the pinnace, although there was armed resistance. Her occupants were transferred to the pinnace and this was allowed to go. The barque was taken as well as one of the three or four pilots who were travelling in her.

Part 2. Testimony of San Juan Antón, whose ship was taken

At noon on Sunday, the first of March, San Juan de Antón, being out at sea in his ship, between the Cape of San Francisco and Galera Point [in Ecuador], saw, close to land, a ship which was going the same way, bound for Panama. He thought she was a barque from Guayaquil and bore toward her. At about nine o'clock at night, the English ship crossed the course of San Juan's vessel and, immediately, came alongside. San Juan saluted but the corsair did not return the salute. Believing her to be a ship from Chile which was then in rebellion, Master Antón came to the side. By that time the English were already grappling his ship shouting: "Englishman! Strike sail!" Someone said: "Strike sail, Mr. Juan de Antón; if not, look out, for you will be sent to the bottom."

San Juan answered: "What England is this which gives me orders for striking sail? Come on board to strike the sails yourselves!" On hearing this they blew the whistle on the English ship and the trumpet responded. Then a volley of what seemed to be about 60 arquebuses was shot, followed by many arrows, which struck the side of the ship, and chain-balls shot from a heavy piece of ordnance carried away the mizzen and sent it into the sea with its sail and lateen yard. After this the English shot another great gun, shouting again: "Strike sail!" and simultaneously, a pinnace laid aboard to port and about 40 archers climbed up the channels of the shrouds and entered San Juan de Antón's ship, while, at the opposite side, the English ship laid aboard. It is thus that they forced San Juan's ship to surrender. They inquired for the pilot and captain from the selfsame San Juan de Antón, who was alone on deck. He would not answer them. Not seeing any other person on deck, they seized him and carried him to the English ship where he saw the corsair Francis Drake, who was removing his helmet and coat of mail. Francis Drake embraced San Juan de Antón, saying: "Have patience, for such is the usage of war," and immediately ordered him to be locked up in the cabin in the poop, with twelve men to guard him.

Part 3. Testimony of Nuño da Silva, Drake's Portuguese pilot, tried by the Inquisition in Mexico City, May 23, 1579

This Englishman calls himself Francis Drake and is a man aged 38.... He is low in stature, thick-set and very robust. He has a fine countenance, is ruddy of complexion and has a fair beard. He has the mark of an arrow wound in his right cheek which is not apparent if one does not look with special care. In one leg he has the ball of an arquebus that was shot at him in the Indies. He is a great mariner, the son and relative of seamen, and particularly of John Hawkins in whose company he was for a long time. He has with him a brother named Thomas Drake who served as a

Francis Drake's *Golden Hind* attacks the Spanish ship *Cacafuego* off
Ecuador, 1579. John Carter Brown Library at Brown University.

sailor, like any one of the crew. Thomas Drake is 22 years of age, has a fair complexion and a scanty beard, which is fair. He is low of stature but is broad-shouldered and sturdy. He is a good seaman. Francis Drake took with him from England, all told, 270 men, amongst whom there were some of whom he made more account and had seated at his table, namely, the captain, pilot, and doctor. He also read the psalms and preached.

Part 4. An anonymous English account, c.1580

We fell with the port of Paita in 4 deg. 40 min. [south latitude], 20 February, with the Port St. Helen and the river and port of Guayaquil, 24 February. We passed the [Equatorial] Line the 28th, and the first of March we fell with the Cape [of San] Francisco, where, about midday, we descried a sail ahead of us, with whom, after once we had spoken with her, we lay still in the same place about six days to recover our breath again, which we had almost spent with hasty following, and to recall to mind what adventures had passed us since our late coming from Lima; but especially to do John de Anton a kindness, in freeing him of the care of those things with which his ship was loaden.

This ship was found to be the same of which we had heard, not only in the Callao [port] of Lima, but also by divers occasions afterwards, which now we are at leisure to relate, viz., by a ship which we took between Lima and Paita; by another, which we took loaden with wine in the port of Paita; by a third, loaden with tackling and implements for ships (besides 80 pounds weight in gold) from Guayaquil. And lastly, by Gabriel Alvarez, with whom we talked somewhat nearer the [Equatorial] Line. We found her to be indeed the *Cacafuego*, though before we left her, she was newly named by a boy of her own the *Cacaplata*. We found in her some fruit, conserves, sugars, meal, and other victuals, and (that which was of the especialist cause of her heavy and slow sailing) a certain quantity of jewels and precious stones, 13 chests of rials of plate, 80 pounds weight in gold, 26 tons of uncoined silver, two very fair gilt silver drinking bowls, and the like trifles, valued in all at about 360,000 pesos. We gave the master a little linen and the like for these commodities, and at the end of six days we bade farewell and parted. He hastening somewhat lighter than before to Panama, we plying off to sea, that we might with more leisure consider what course henceforward were fittest to be taken.

DOCUMENT 10

Francis Drake to Philip II of Spain: 'Don't Call Me a Pirate!' (1586)[6]

Writing in what is today highland Colombia in the late 1580s, poet Juan de Castellanos included in his epic poem Elegies to the Illustrious Men of the Indies *a section on Francis Drake, specifically his 1586 sack of Cartagena de Indias, Spain's major port on the Caribbean coast of South America. Castellanos knew and interviewed several of the city's Spanish defenders. Apparently concerned that the poem misrepresented royal policy against a known pirate, and furthermore a Protestant heretic, Spain's Inquisition censors excised the Drake sequence, consisting of 715 stanzas. The manuscript, sliced from the original, was rediscovered in 1886. "His Majesty" refers to King Philip II, whom Drake had declared an enemy well before England went to war with Spain in 1585. According to Castellanos, why was Drake allegedly upset at being called a pirate?*

The conversations [between Drake and Spain's royal officials]
    continued
Lacking any true advantage
And the Englishman justifying
Always favoring his right
Unable to hide the passions
Bottled up in his proud breast
Because His Majesty had treated him badly
By putting upon him the name of pirate.

And he said: 'I well know how such a grand
And potent sovereign monarch
May not always be able to read the thing
That is placed before his hand to sign;
Trusting the generous people,

---

6. Source: Juan de Castellanos, *Discurso de el Capitán Francisco Draque*, ed. Ángel González Palencia (Madrid: Instituto de Valencia de Don Juan, 1921), 208–9. (Translation Kris Lane, with thanks to Timothy F. Johnson.)

The worlds furuaied bounds, braue Drake on thee did gaze,
Both North and Southerne Poles, haue seene thy manly face.
If thankleße men conceale, thy prayse the starres woulde blaze,
The Sunne his fellow-trauellers worth will duely grace.
Ro: Vaughan sculp

Portrait of Sir Francis Drake from *The World Encompassed*,
1628. John Carter Brown Library at Brown University.

The loyal and trusted courtier;
And this decree was in this way
Signed, without reading what it said.

'To whatever sir who invented this
Base word [pirate], should he write me,
The reply won't be long in coming
Because I will surely unmask the lie
With an addition no less insolent
That will fully satisfy me
Yet I trust God that I'll see myself in Spain
And in this matter I'll be redressed.

'And there we'll make it clear one day
So that I may be vindicated
Before the Great Philip who sent it
By the secretaries in whom he confided.'
These and many other things he said
With a fierce look and a reddened face
But these things he treated only showed that he was touched
With near madness by his victories.

DOCUMENT 11

Francisco de Sande, "The Pirate Limahon attacks Manila" (1574)[7]

Dr. Francisco de Sande was one of the first Spanish governors of Manila, capital of the Philippines and Spain's most significant Asian colony. The city and part of the surrounding island of Luzon were conquered beginning in 1565 by forces sent from Mexico under Miguel López de Legazpi, and many Philippine islanders remained entirely outside Spanish control. Sande's

---

7. Source: Filibiniana Book Guild, ed., *The Colonization and Conquest of the Philippines by Spain: Some Contemporary Source Documents, 1559–1577*, intr. Rafael Bernal (Manila: FBG, 1965), 294–303.

report of the 1574 attack of the corsair Limahon (Lin Feng) serves as a reminder of how fragile Spanish control of even its most important Asian trading city was at this early date. How close did Lin Feng come to capturing Manila, and why did he retreat, according to this chronicler?

I learned in these islands [on my way here from Mexico] that this city had been burned by a pirate and that there had been a war. . . . On my arrival, I found Manila in great part burned and destroyed. . . . They say that the kingdom of China is often invaded by corsairs, and that one named Limahon had committed great depredations in China, whereby he had great wealth. He was pursued by his king to the region near the upper point of the island of Luzon. Near an island about 40 leagues from Luzon, he captured a Chinese merchant ship that was en route from this city of Manila for purposes of trade. The merchants carried with them a quantity of gold and many Mexican half-pesos, and other things obtained in this island, which were highly esteemed by them. Demanding with threats where they had obtained this gold and silver, he robbed them of their goods, which they said had been obtained in Luzon in trade with the Castilians. . . . On the way, however, at dawn of day, without himself being seen, he met one of your Majesty's galliots. . . . When the corsair saw the galliot, he lowered his small boats and made an assault upon it . . .

With this prize captured . . . the corsair proceeded toward Manila . . . and, intending to make an attack at dawn, anchored outside the bay. . . . They say that the corsair remained with the ships; but that in the boats there were 700 men, among whom were a few arquebusiers, and many pikemen, besides men armed with battle axes. They were clad in corselets which are coats lined with exceedingly thick cotton. They had durable bamboo hats, which served as helmets; they carried cutlasses and several daggers in their belts, and all were barefoot. Their manner of warfare or of fighting was to form a squadron composed of men with battle-axes, among whom were placed some arquebusiers, a few of the latter going ahead as skirmishers. One of every ten men carried a banner, fastened to his shoulders and reaching two palms above his head . . .

They did not enter by the river, in order not to be seen by the fishermen who are constantly going and coming. . . . The pirates therefore began a hurried march along the shore toward the city, dragging their lances. They arrived at the city somewhere between nine and ten o'clock in the morning. The first house attacked was that of the field marshal, Martin de Goite; he was sick in bed at the time. Already some native Filipinos had come to him from the shore, shouting at the tops of their voices that enemies were near, and that the king of Borneo was coming down upon the Castilians. Now as Martin de Goite knew that this was the season of the monsoon, and that it was impossible to come from Borneo, which lies to the southwest, because the wind was dead ahead, and not believing in the possibility of other enemies, he laughed at the men, telling them they were drunk. Meanwhile, the advance guard of the squadron was near the house when he arose, put on a suit of mail, and took a sword with which to defend himself. It is believed that the Chinese were passing straight ahead toward the governor's house and the artillery, guided by the spy whom they brought with them, for they were stealing along the shore forward . . .

It is said that when the enemies came marching in line along the seacoast, the wife of field marshal Martin de Goite was looking out of a window that faced the seacoast. She had a child's helmet on her head, and she called and beckoned to them in Castilian that they were dogs, and that they would all be killed. The Chinese observed this, and learned from the guide that this was the house of the field marshal. They regarded this as a very important piece of news, and going to that house hurled many fire bombs, with which they burned it in a very short time; for it was made, like all the houses there, of wood and straw. They killed some men who had gathered there; they also killed the field marshal, who had been injured by the fire and wounded by an arquebus shot in the arm, and who threw himself from a window on account of the cruel flames. . . . Several other persons were killed there with him. His wife, who had shouted to them, they stripped and tore off a ring that she was slow in drawing from her finger, and a necklace; and then they stabbed her severely in the neck. She rushed from the house and hid in the tall grass, thus escaping with her life, and she is now alive. . . . When the affair of the house was over, the pirates attempted to proceed once more to the beach.

The delay at the house was important, for in the meanwhile Captains Velázquez and Chacón, with what soldiers there were, went to the seacoast; and from the shelter of the houses facing the beach fired well-aimed volleys from their arquebuses, whereat a number of Limahon's advance guard fell. Thus was God pleased that with the death of thirteen or fourteen Spaniards and more than 80 Chinese, the latter had enough, retreated to their boats, and went away. The Spaniards did not molest them while they were retreating on this day on account of their own small number of fighting men, and for fear that such a course might incite those fleeing to return. The corsairs did not utter a word, nor did they complain, even when they fell with wounds. Those in command endeavored to induce their men to press forward, but did not succeed ...

The corsairs went to the port of Cavite, where they found their chief with all their fleet; for on seeing the fire in the city and hearing the roar of the artillery, he knew that his men were accomplishing their purpose, and entered the bay, going straight to the port of Cavite. Those of his men who had gone to the city in the boats told him they were unable to finish the affair or to accomplish more, for the Castilians were a very brave people.

After the flight of the Chinese, a Chinese merchant who was in the city, Sinsay by name, called upon the governor. He told him the corsair's name, who he was, and his power. He also stated that he was a pirate, and not sent by the order of his king; and that without doubt he would return in three days. He advised the Spaniards to fortify themselves, and to remove the straw from the roofs of your Majesty's buildings, so that they could not be fired—advice which was acted upon.

The corsair Limahon rebuked his captains, and publicly manifested his disgust at their defeat. Then he summoned his soldiers, paid them all, and made them great promises. They agreed to rest one day and to return in the morning of the third day, when he would accompany them personally—which he did, with his entire fleet.

The first attack was made on the day of St. Andrew the Apostle. On Tuesday, the last of September of the year 1574, the captains began the fortifications, making with boards, stakes, and boxes and barrels filled with sand a palisade from the river to the sea. Although it was the best they could build, it was weak enough. The next day, Wednesday, at noon three soldiers came to warn the people. . . . Very early on the next day [Thursday] the Chinese advanced in martial array, as if determined upon revenge. At four o'clock the whole fleet appeared in front of the city in the form of a great crescent, so that they might be there before daybreak; and three salutes were fired from all the guns of the whole fleet. Then at dawn they lowered the small boats, finally disembarking near the house of the field marshal, which they had burned. The chief Limahon landed, but it is reported that he did not fight, or leave that place, where he remained seated in a chair. He divided his soldiers there—numbering, it is said, about 1,000 men—into two bodies. Part of them he sent through the principal street of the city, and the others along the beach. The latter took the same route as those who arrived on the first day. Besides these two squadrons, other men were sent along the riverbank . . .

This day the pirates, as if previously determined, did not burn any houses that seemed to be of good quality. They went straight to the fort, and assailed it vigorously on two sides. They encountered a strong resistance from the riverside and in front, and some of them were killed. On the side next to the sea the guard of the fort was entrusted to a sergeant named Sancho Ortiz de Agurto. He went down to the shore, leaving his post, where he was stationed to find out from what quarter the Chinese were coming. They were already so near that, upon one of the Chinese meeting him, the lance of the latter must have proved the longer weapon; for he wounded [Ortiz de Agurto], who was armed only with a halberd, in the neck. Either this wound or some other obliged him to retire, and upon doing so the Chinese shot him in the back with an arquebus, which caused his death . . .

On this account it happened that when [Lin Feng's soldiers] forced that position, they found there the least resistance. About 80 Chinese entered the fort at that point, and all of them might have done so had they been of equal courage. Our soldiers attacked them immediately with lance and arquebus, killing them all, according to report. The result was aided by the resistance experienced by the assaulters in other parts of the fort, which forced the Chinese to commence a retreat. Now when the main division of those who had entered the fort saw the others retreat, they too retreated and did not enter, abandoning the 80, all of whom the Spaniards killed whether they sought flight by land or sea. On this day they burned the Augustinian church, the [central parish] church of the city, and a galley that was grounded near the river; and they also destroyed an old ship. . . . The greatest damage was caused by the fire, for a great fire-bomb fell upon some powder, which exploded causing the death of two or three other men.

It is said that the corsair Limahon tried to force his men to remain, but was unsuccessful, so he retired, embarked in his boats, and set sail with his vessels for the port of Cavite. . . . They say that the corsair had, in all, about 3,000 men and as many women, whom he had forcibly taken from China and Japan. The best people that he had were natives of those countries.

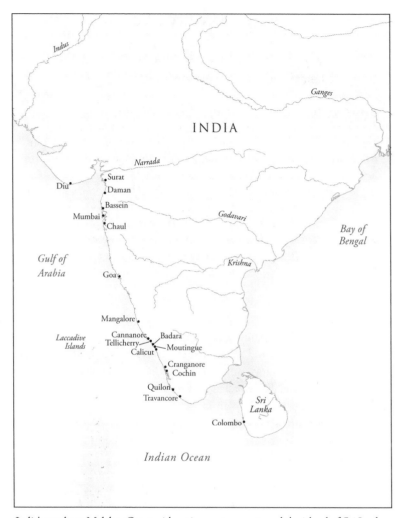

India's southern Malabar Coast with major western ports and the island of Sri Lanka.

DOCUMENT 12

The Pirates of India's Malabar Coast Described by Pyrard de Laval (c.1601)[8]

Between 1601 and 1611 the French navigator François Pyrard de Laval visited South Asia and nearby island chains such as the Maldives. A keen if not always reliable observer, Pyrard took extensive notes and subsequently published a book about his adventures. As a Frenchman traveling in regions where maritime trade was technically monopolized by the Portuguese but in reality was contested by various other nations and groups, Pyrard's notes are of special interest. His account includes a description of the so-called Malabari pirates that were active on the southwest coast of India throughout the seventeenth century. Notice how Pyrard depicts the Malabaris and their sponsors, and how he describes the distribution of booty.

As I have said, my companions and I embarked in a ship of Calicut; we were at sea three weeks, and at length made land at the port of Moutingue, which is situate between Cannanore and Calicut: it is one of the harbors of refuge for the Malabar corsairs and pirates. The country is under the king of Moutingue, who is a Nair king.

I was never more astonished than on my arrival there to see so many men-at-arms: everyone there carries arms, as well Mahometans as idolaters, from the age of ten or twelve—that is, all the Nairs or Malabars, for the villain [peasant] folk carry none at all. I was received with great courtesy by the Malabars while I sojourned there. I was conducted to the house of a great lord, a Mahometan Malabar. . . . [Although] the country belongs to the Malabars, yet in speaking of the Malabars, the Mahometans are more properly intended. They are but seldom artisans, almost all being merchants, robbers, or sea warriors. There is no class of nobles among them; their distinction is solely in valor and wealth, and all sorts of men are welcomed among them. They but seldom keep slaves, and none are constrained to go to the wars with them. They are trustful

---

8. Source: Pyrard de Laval, *The Voyage of Francois Pyrard of Laval to the East Indies, the Maldives, the Moluccas and Brazil,* 2 vols. (New York: Burt Franklin, 1963), vol. 1, 336–38.

toward all men, and care not to compel others to go where they go. They provide a free table for all comers, and each has his own dish: that is, all soldiers. All their people are employed, for such as are not brave enough for soldiers, they make mariners, or press them into service for hire, or use them for selling the produce of their robberies.

Their galliots they call *pados*. All the merchants of the coast, when they hear that the galliots of the pirates are about to come in, hold themselves in readiness to buy their goods cheap, and then they have the assurance to go and sell them in the markets of the very merchants of whom they were taken. These latter frequently buy them back a second time; and though they recognize their own goods, that matters not, so long as they have the Portuguese passport.

The priests of their religion, too, and the poor are on the look-out, and come distances of 30 leagues to get their share; for they well know that these Malabars have made vows, in case they make a good prize, to give so much to the poor, and never fail to acquit themselves therein . . .

These robbers must take great booty, for besides the cost and expenses of their *pados* and galliots, they have to pay customs and passport duties to the Nair king of the land; then they are subjected to the giving of all sorts of gratifications and presents—as, for instance, to the king of Calicut and to their own king. . . . They have to give to their allies; and finally, to their priests and the poor, and in fulfillment of vows . . .

When they set out for war, and for a round of expeditions, they appoint a general of the whole fleet whom they obey during that voyage only; when it is over he returns to his former position. If any prize is taken, they give him a present, as they may be minded, though he has no right thereto; the rest is equally divided . . .

It is impossible to describe in detail the welcome and good friendship extended to us by the Malabar Mahometans and Nairs. They counted themselves lucky when they got us under their roofs, saying that God had greatly blessed them; and most of them put in writing the day and hour of our coming in, and told their children to remember the day they saw us. All ran out upon the road to see us when they heard tell of our name, and how that we were enemies to the Portuguese. . . . The Portuguese have done all they know to conquer these four towns and ports, but always without effect, and to their own loss and discredit, chiefly so at Badara, where they have lost many of their men; for it is an exceeding strong port, all surrounded with water. They got soundly beaten there only a month before my arrival.

QUESTIONS TO CONSIDER FOR SECTION II:

How and where did piracy in the sixteenth-century Atlantic typically occur?

What role did contraband trade play in encouraging piracy in the Caribbean?

How did sixteenth-century piracy in the South China Sea and the Indian Ocean compare?

SECTION III: PIRATES OF THE MEDITERRANEAN

Merchant vessels and vulnerable towns were on the minds of all ambitious pirates, but in the Mediterranean the peculiarities of geography and shared history gave rise to a special kind of piracy by early modern times. After the Ottomans captured Istanbul in 1453, maritime conflict between Christians and Muslims increased in tandem with the volume of trade. Eastern demand for Western silver was matched by Western demand for Eastern luxuries such as silk and spices. Having seized the main conduits of Asian trade, the Ottomans nurtured clients in North Africa who harried Christian shippers just as the Habsburgs and other Christian powers sponsored sea raiders such as the Knights of St. John and St. Stephen. Concentrated in this well-traveled and compact "sea between the lands," Mediterranean piracy evolved into a remarkably intimate system of raiding, ransoming, extortion, and diplomacy. The so-called Barbary or "Berber" corsairs of North Africa deftly played European powers against one another. As Ottoman sea power declined after 1571, when their navy was destroyed in the battle of Lepanto, the Europeans attempted to reverse the process, playing corsairs and their sponsors against one another in Morocco, Algeria, Tunisia, and Libya. The following selection of documents offers a taste of the peculiar "pirate culture" that emerged in the sixteenth-century Mediterranean and lasted until the second decade of the nineteenth century.

DOCUMENT 13 (IN TWO PARTS)

Life among the Corsairs of Algiers (c.1581)[1]

In 1577 a Portuguese priest educated in Spain and serving in Sicily was captured by Algiers-based corsairs while sailing from Barcelona to Valeta, capital of Malta. Although his account of

---

1. Source: Diego de Haedo [pen name of Antonio de Sosa], *Topographia e historia general de Argel* (Valladolid: Diego Fernández de Córdoba y Oviedo, 1612), 15v–18v. (Available online.) (Translation Kris Lane.)

The Mediterranean Basin with key ports, islands, and cities from the great age of piracy.

captivity was published many years later under another name, Antonio de Sosa left a rich account of life in what was arguably the Mediterranean's corsair capital in the later sixteenth century. While in captivity in the so-called bagnos of Algiers, Sosa penned a detailed description of the city and its inhabitants, along with a history of its leaders and a formal dialogue explaining the situation of captives. One feature that stands out in Sosa's account is the remarkable diversity of corsairs and other inhabitants of late-sixteenth century Algiers. Sosa's description is not without bias, and may have been intended to help raise funds for the so-called Redemptionist Orders, the Mercedarians and Trinitarians who collected alms from all over the Spanish empire to free "Barbary captives." Redeemed for the sizeable sum of 1,500 escudos in 1581, Sosa met fellow captive Miguel de Cervantes, a then unknown Spanish veteran who would later become Spain's most renowned fiction writer. Cervantes included reflections on his time in captivity in Don Quijote and other works.

Part 1. On the corsairs of Algiers, their customs and habits

The corsairs are those who live to rob continuously at sea, and it is notable that although there are some among them of the Turkish nation as well as some Moors, almost all of them are renegades of every nation, all quite skilled in navigating the estuaries, ports, and coasts of Christendom. The vessels they use to go corsairing are light galliots, or brigantines, which they call frigates. The brigantine has eight to thirteen banks of oars, and the galliot from fourteen to twenty-four. These vessels are built constantly in Algiers, partly in the shipyards set aside for this, and partly on the island in the middle of the city's port, connected to it by the pier's embankment ...

Most corsair captains have shipbuilders in their households, in part because when they capture a Christian ship these are the captives they seek, or wish to buy at high cost. And it is such that without the Christian tradesmen the Turks might not have a single ship among them ...

The number of soldiers and armed men they go out with depends on the ship, and here is the rule: against each bank of oars above the portholes is a bench or wooden seat, upon which sit two soldiers, such that if a galliot has twenty oars or benches per side, multiplying the benches, with two rowers a piece, there are twice as many soldiers as oars. These soldiers are either janissaries who go corsairing with license from their *agha* or renegades. A few are Turks who live only by this trade, and all the soldiers of the sea are commonly called Levanters.

None of these have any salary or means of gain beyond what they can steal. They must pool funds, and to do so they band together in groups of ten, twelve, or more. Even so, the captain and outfitters are obligated to give them biscuit, oil, and vinegar, rationed according to the number of Christian rowers. Each vessel typically carries biscuit, rice, bulgur wheat, oil, vinegar, cheese, rendered fat, olives, and some dried fruit, nothing more. The daily ration they grant to those who row, and to all the Levanters and the crew of the ship is a little biscuit, some watered-down vinegar, a few spoonsful of oil, and to the Christians they often give nothing but biscuit.

They must leave the port of Algiers on either Friday, which is their holy day, or Sunday, that of the Christians, and they do not set out except in the dark of night. Before weighing anchor and leaving the port every vessel, whether corsair or merchant, salutes the tomb of a dead imam whom they regard as a saint, and it is outside the port of Bab 'Azzun in a cave like an underground chapel known as Sidi Batqa. And all of them turning toward it, they say in a loud voice, ordering the Christians to do so as well, "a la hora, a la hora," which means, "in the name of God, in the name of God . . ."

They go corsairing all through the summer and winter, sailing fearlessly throughout the eastern and western seas, making light of the Christian galleys, often because their crews are feasting, gambling, and carrying on in the ports of Christendom. Meanwhile they go hunting as if to take so many hares and rabbits, killing one here, and there another. It is understood that their galliots are swift, disciplined, and light, whereas the Christian galliots are heavy, and so disorderly and encumbered that they may as well give the others license to hunt, to block the sea-lanes as they like and pillage at pleasure. And it is such that when the Christian galleys give chase, they make fun of them, mocking them, "showing them the grease" while moving off and fleeing, as if to moon them. And they are so dexterous in the art of corsairing, and so experienced—and by our sins made brave and fortunate—that a few days after leaving Algiers they return loaded with infinite riches and captives. And in the space of a year they can make three or four voyages, and as many more as they wish should they prepare quickly . . .

They pay great attention to the cleanliness, order, and harmony of their vessels that they hardly go over or think of anything else, most importantly that they have everything properly stowed, so as to sail swiftly and with great prowess, and for this purpose their ships do not have gunwales, nor do they let a single sword or arquebus hang from the sides, nor lie on deck uncovered, but rather all are placed in stowage. In the same manner they stow the barrels and jugs of oil, vinegar, and grease, with all the rest of the provisions and materiel battened down flat, without a single thing moving a fingernail's width from its place. They are so concerned about this that some even stow their anchor below decks, since having it above throws off the vessel's weight distribution. And finally, for this same reason they do not allow any Turk, Levanter, or Christian to move from his assigned spot, even if he is the very son of the king . . .

Of the booty they take, which they call *ghanima*, including captives and commodities, all belong to the ship's captain himself, the lord of the vessel, along with those who helped him outfit it, and the same with any money or jewels they might take or steal. But in these latter things they do not proceed with the same rigor, unless it is some great prize famed for its cargo of money. Unless this is the case, the Levanters are left with all the money they can find and easily conceal. All the clothing and garments they take belong to the Levanters and soldiers, the same having a good custom, which is to share out equally among themselves as if all had stolen it personally. If they fight with a vessel that does not wish to surrender, the Turk who boards first and forces it to surrender gets first choice of all the Christians on board, taking the one he likes most as long as he is not worth too much in ransom.

If they sack some town or village, the captain and outfitters pay ten escudos for each Christian captive they embark. And if a ship does surrender without a fight, no one gets any captives, only their clothes and whatever else they might be able to pilfer. The hulls and timbers of the ship belong to the king. They understand that the seventh part of all captives, however chosen, and of all clothing taken, or money stolen, or of whatever commodity they may have, belongs to the king in whose port the vessel was outfitted and manned for that voyage. And if they should go out corsairing a second time having been outfitted in another place, this tribute would belong to its king. And thus is the custom of Algiers, Tunis, and Tripoli . . .

Upon reaching port after their corsairing voyage, just as they cease rowing and drop anchor, all the Christians push their oars out into the water, remaining tied up only by a thin strand or rope. And once debarked, some or all, the first thing they do is take the oars to be stored in a public warehouse that is right next to the port, where these are carefully guarded. They do this so that when the Turks go ashore with their booty the Christians do not mutiny and take off in the vessel. And afterwards that same day they collect and take home their Christians, and at that point the captains and Levanters all begin to spend most liberally, hosting great banquets that they call *sofras*, and buying wine and *raki*, which is fire water, and on all manner of luxuries they spend all that they have stolen on the voyage. And thus all of Algiers is contented, since the merchants purchase many slaves and commodities that the corsairs have brought in, and the tradesmen of the city sell whatever they have in their shops, be it clothing or supplies, to those who have come back from the sea, as many buy new outfits. And all is eating, drinking, and cheering . . .

Part 2. Catalogue of corsairs

The following corsairs were based in Algiers in 1581. Some would send out their vessels with substitutes when they themselves did not sail.

1. King Dja'far, Hungarian renegade, one of 24 benches
2. Mami Arnaut [Arnault], sea captain, renegade, one of 22 benches
3. Murad the French, renegade of the captain [above], one of 22 benches
4. Dali Mami, Greek renegade, one of 22 benches
5. Murad Ra'is the Great, Albanian renegade, one of 24 benches
6. Feru Ra'is, Genoese renegade, one of 18 benches
7. Murad Ra'is, "Maltrapillo," Spanish renegade, one of 22 benches
8. 'Isa Ra'is, of the Turkish nation, one of 18 benches
9. Arapsa Ra'is, of the Turkish nation, one of 18 benches
10. Amiça Ra'is, Turk, one of 20 benches
11. Little Murad Ra'is, Greek renegade, one of 18 benches
12. Sinan Ra'is, Turk, one of 22 benches
13. Yusuf Ra'is, Spanish renegade, one of 22 benches,
14. Hadjdji Bali, Turk, one of 18 benches
15. Hasan, Genoese, renegade belonging to the imam, one of 18 benches
16. El Ka'id Dawud, Turk, one of 20 benches
17. El Ka'id Khader, son of a renegade, one of 23 benches
18. El Ka'id Giger, Turk, one of 22 benches

19. Marja Mami, Genoese renegade, one of 18 benches
20. Mamixa, Turk, one of 18 benches
21. El Ka'id Muhammad, of the Jewish nation, one of 15 benches
22. Mamixa, Genoese renegade, one of 18 benches
23. Mami Ra'is, Venetian renegade, one of 22 benches
24. Mami Gancho, Venetian renegade, one of 20 benches
25. Mami Corso, Corsican renegade, one of 20 benches
26. Mami Calabrés, Calabrian renegade, one of 20 benches
27. Paduan Ra'is, son of a renegade, one of 22 benches
28. Kadi Ra'is, Turk, one of 22 benches
29. Dondardi, Greek renegade, one of 19 benches
30. Dja'far Montez, Sicilian renegade of Trapani, one of 22 benches
31. Hasan the Baker, Genoese renegade, one of 15 benches
32. Kari Ra'is, Turk, one of 18 benches
33. Kaur 'Ali, son of a renegade, one of 20 benches
34. Yusuf Remolar, Neapolitan renegade, one of 20 benches
35. Dja'far, Genoese renegade, one of 20 benches

DOCUMENT 14

A Letter from Barbary (1630)[2]

The following letter, translated from the Arabic and now housed in the British Library, provides a rare window on diplomacy between the ruler of Morocco and the king of England, Charles I. In dictating the letter, the Moroccan ruler did not overtly mention piracy or corsair activity for diplomatic reasons, but an aim of this formal overture was to minimize attacks on shipping while shoring up alliances against the Spanish and Portuguese—that is, to play European powers against one another. Mediterranean captive exchange involved the highly formalized presentation of these letters, which sometimes emphasized religious difference and broader notions of dominion that left the Mediterranean to serve as frontier.

---

2. Source: J. F. P. Hopkins, ed. and trans. *Letters from Barbary, 1576–1774* (Oxford: Oxford University Press, 1982), 7.

Abu 'l-Hasan Ali b. Muhammad to
Charles I, September 16, 1630

Your letter has reached our lofty Abode giving thanks for our treatment of the prisoners your companions who came out to this region, since we were good enough to release them from captivity. This was done by us out of solicitude for the interests of Islam, so that there may not remain in all your territory a single Muslim captive except you send him out to the land of Islam, whether he be one of the people of our country or another of the countries of Islam; likewise any who may be outside your jurisdiction, if you find some way to obtain his release. If you are faithful in this then we grant you security in your property and persons in conformity with the pact that was made between certain former princes of Islam and yourself. We have renewed this pact with you to the same effect so that no captive from the tribes of England will remain with us as long as you remain in fulfillment of the pact, making your best efforts therein. Eight nights have elapsed of the month of Safar in the year 1040 of the Prophet's emigration.

DOCUMENT 15

The Ransom Receipt of Miguel de Cervantes (1580)[3]

The ransom note of Miguel de Cervantes, who later became Spain's most famous fiction writer, was found in an account book belonging to the Trinitarian Redemptionist Order. The Trinitarians and Mercedarians raised money all over Spain and its empire to release Christian captives held by the so-called Barbary corsairs. In this case, Cervantes' ransom was to be paid only in gold, here exchanged beforehand by the redemptionists for Spanish silver pieces of eight. Otherwise, Cervantes was probably a typical captive. A wounded veteran of the battle of Lepanto, he was decades away from being a celebrity.

---

3. Source: María Antonia Garcés, *Cervantes in Algiers: A Captive's Tale* (Nashville: Vanderbilt University Press, 2002), 109–10.

In the city of Algiers, on the 19th day of September [of 1580], in my presence, as the said notary, the very reverend Fray Juan Gil, the said Redemptionist, ransomed Miguel de Cervantes, native of Alcalá de Henares, 31 years old, son of Rodrigo de Cervantes and doña Leonor de Cortinas, residents in the city of Madrid, medium-bodied, well bearded, crippled in his left arm and hand, captured in the galley *Sol*, sailing from Naples to Spain. . . . He was lost on 26 September 1575. He was in the hands of Hasan Pasha, king. His ransom cost 500 gold escudos [paid] in gold. His master did not want to free him if he was not paid with gold escudos, in Spanish gold, otherwise he would have taken him to Constantinople. . . . Cervantes was helped by the charity of Francisco de Caramanchel . . . with 50 pieces of eight. And from the general charity of the [Redemptionist] Order he was helped with another 50. As for the rest, in complying with the 1,340 pieces of eight, he signed an obligation to pay them to the said Order, because these are coins destined for other captives whose families in Spain gave the money for their rescue, and because they are not presently in Algiers, they have not been rescued . . .

DOCUMENT 16

Miguel de Cervantes' Captive Fantasies of the Golden Age (1615)[4]

The following passage is taken from the play The Great Sultana *by Miguel de Cervantes, written in 1615. As we have seen, Cervantes had considerable experience as a young man among the corsairs of Algiers, who held him captive for five years. Captive tales were nothing new when Cervantes wrote, but his personal experiences and skills as a writer rendered stock villains as ambivalent characters, constantly questioning the meaning of cultural, racial, and even gendered borders. Even so, Cervantes*

4. Source: Miguel de Cervantes, *The Bagnios of Algiers and The Great Sultana: Two Plays of Captivity*, ed. and trans. Barbara Fuchs and Aaron J. Ilika (Philadelphia: University of Pennsylvania Press, 2010), 154–55.

*could not resist the trope of the valiant Christian maiden whose
virtue in captivity could not be broken by the Ottoman sultan
himself. Such was the fictional Catalina de Oviedo, a.k.a. The
Great Sultana.*

A certain so-and-so from Oviedo embarked one winter from Málaga for
Oran on a ship of ten oars. He was a gentleman, but not a rich one: that's
the curse of our times, for it seems that being poor and being an hidalgo
are one and the same thing. His wife and daughter, young and extremely
beautiful, went with him too. The sea promised a fast crossing, as it was
January, the time when corsairs retire to their ports; but since misfortunes sail in all weather, such a grave one befell them that they lost their
liberty. [The corsair] Morato Arráez, who doesn't sleep in order to keep
us from rest, caught up with the light ship in that crossing; he stopped in
Tetuán and sold the girl straightaway to a famous and rich Moor named
Ali Izquierdo.

The girl's mother died of grief; they brought her father to Algiers,
where his old age saved him from rowing in the galleys. Four years passed
when Morato, back in Tetuán, beheld the girl, more lovely than the sun
itself. He bought her from his patron, paying Ali eight times what he had
paid for her in the first place. Ali told Morato: 'I'm happy to sell her, for I
can't turn her Turk with gifts or pleas. She's only ten years old, but so wise
in her years that they trump old men's mature ones. She's the glory of her
nation and an exemplar of fortitude, all the more so as she's alone, and of
the lesser and fragile sex.' The great corsair, overjoyed with his purchase,
came to Constantinople in the year 1600, I believe; he presented her to
the [Ottoman Sultan, the] Great Signor, a young lad at the time, who
immediately handed her over to the eunuchs of the seraglio. They tried
to change her sweet name, Catalina, to Zoraida; but she never consented,
nor her last name, de Oviedo. Finally, after some time the Great Signor
saw her, and as if beholding the sun, was rendered lifeless and amazed;
he offered her the inheritance of his extensive kingdoms, and gave her his
soul as a sign . . .

DOCUMENT 17

The Corsair Alonso de Contreras
Tells His Tale (1630)[5]

*Alonso de Contreras was a Spanish soldier who traveled widely
in the Mediterranean in the early seventeenth century. His many
exploits, recounted in a 1630 autobiography, included corsair
raids ordered by the Knights of St. John of Malta. This multinational military-religious order mirrored the Barbary corsairs,
engaging in long-distance raids, captive exchange, and other violent acts under the auspices of religious and imperial struggle.
As historians have recently shown, the Knights of St. John and
St. Stephen (based in Livorno, near Pisa) also attacked "soft" targets, including merchant vessels sent out by Orthodox Christian
Greeks who lived under Ottoman rule. Attacking the Barbary corsairs directly was a much riskier endeavor, as Contreras relates in
this self-aggrandizing narrative of events off the coast of modern
Libya.*

I continued my voyage back to Barbary that night and awoke near the
sandbank of El Seco, ten miles out from Tripoli, where we encountered
a galliot with seventeen banks of oars, which I was not happy to see. As
they spotted me, they hoisted a green banner with three crescent moons
that hung down to the water line. My people became dismayed and the
skipper said: "Oh my, we're all slaves, it's the galliot of the Ka'id Mami of
Tripoli." I laughed and said "Look, friends, we've got a great prize today." I
stopped and didn't move the ship as a precaution. I got my culverin ready
and filled it with nails, lead, and crushed rock and I said: "Leave it to me,
as this galliot is ours for the taking; each of you get out your swords and
bucklers, and soldiers: grab your muskets." We had eight Spanish soldiers
whom I trusted.

I headed straight toward the galliot. She sat still, which was good since
I could no longer flee, despite those arguing that I should do so. Turn-
ing back would have been my total ruin, on top of infamy. I told them:
"Friends, don't you see that we're 120 miles from Christian territory

5. Source: Alonso de Contreras, *Discurso de mi vida*, ed. Henry Ettinghausen (Madrid:
Espasa Calpe, 1988), 98–100. (Translation Kris Lane.)

and that this ship is doubly manned and would be upon us in four oar strokes; where's the valor in fleeing? Let me give it a try, as long as I'm alive. Look, as we go to board her, pull alongside and we'll discharge the muskets; they'll duck to receive the barrage." I then promised that when they rose to give us their reply, I would blast them with the culverin I had in my charge.

They thought this was good, and hoisting our colors I went forth with all valor to take advantage of the moment and leave them astonished. And seeing my resolution, as we were already close, she tried to flee. I followed her for more than four hours without being able to catch her, so I ordered my people not to row and to stop and eat. The galliot did the same without pulling away. I turned to give chase and they turned to receive it until evening, when I repeated, pausing again as she did the same.

I kept still all evening and all night, always on guard to see if she would take off under cover of darkness, so that I could continue my voyage to La Cantara. Before dawn I had my people eat, also giving them all the straight wine I could offer, and as dawn broke we had them an arquebus shot away. I pointed the prow at them and as we got close I let fly the musketry. They gripped their oars in fleeing and I in pursuit. I did not want to let them go until I ran them aground in front of the fort of Gelves, where they jumped ashore in water up to their waists, as this is all shallows, and although they fired some cannon at me this did not stop me from attaching a hawser line and hauling her back out where the artillery [of the fort] would not reach me.

Two Christians had remained aboard ship, both slaves, one a Mallorcan and the other a Sicilian from Trapani. There were a few small things aboard, such as shotguns, bows and arrows, and a bit of clothing. I took down her sails and banner and the ship, full of things I did not want to carry on my frigate, I ordered burned. I left and went back toward La Cantara, where I found not a single vessel at the docks. I forgot to mention where the galliot was from; she was from Santa Maura and coming to Barbary to arm herself as a corsair.

From La Cantara I left for Tripoli and in an inlet twelve miles out I struck sail for a whole day and night, and the next day at dawn there passed a small vessel carrying crockery and seventeen Moorish men and women. Not a single one escaped and I put them in my frigate. I sank their vessel after removing a large clay jar full of saffron plus some heavy woolen cloth. I returned to Malta where I was well received. They gave me what I deserved for the slaves, which the Knights of St. John purchased for sixty escudos a piece, whether in good or bad shape, plus a bounty of seven percent for the booty I seized. I happily spent my share with my friends and my mistress, and it was she who got most of what I had won with so much effort.

DOCUMENT 18

An English Diplomat Describes the Corsairs at Tripoli (c.1680)[6]

Thomas Baker served as English consul in Tripoli from 1679 to 1685, during which time he kept a journal. Like the Dutch, the English shifted from open confrontation to diplomacy with the Barbary corsairs in the seventeenth century. The Spanish retreated by the 1630s, just as the French advanced. Baker notes that French aggression against Tripoli and Algiers was only occasionally successful. Everyone else, including the war-weary Venetians and Genoese, had to deal with corsairing by paying ransoms and trying not to get caught. Alongside the comings and goings of Tripoli's corsairs, Baker notes the continuance of ordinary commerce, often with ships flying the same colors as many of those taken and ransomed as prizes. The "dollars" he refers to were typically Spanish American silver pesos or pieces of eight.

10th April [1680]. This day begins the third year of my administration in this place where the damages that have accrued to the navigation of Christendom by the depredations of these corsairs for twelve months past amounts to the several sums listed below:

A barque laden with charcoal sold for Dollars	$500
A French ship, the *Saint Esprit*, and its cargo	$100,000
A great brigantine	$13,000
A West Frenchman	$8,000

6. Source: C. Richard Pennell, ed., *Piracy and Diplomacy in Seventeenth-Century North Africa: The Journal of Thomas Baker, English Consul in Tripoli, 1677–1685* (Cranbury, NJ: Associated University Presses, 1989), 128–30.

A Massigliano, or Venetian Owl	$1,500
A Genoese ship	$3,500
A small ship of Ragusa	$1,500
A Genoese barque	$1,600
A Genoese ship	$25,000
A Maltese ship	$8,000
A barque	$800
A French ship, Capt. Reynard Bon	$100,000
A French ship, Capt. Bartolomeo Ramian	$40,000
A French ship in her ballast	$1,500
A Venetian ship	$10,000
The *America* of Marseilles	$30,000
Capt. Moralio of Marseilles	$10,000
A ship of Ragusa	<u>$5,000</u>
The total of the vessels and goods for 341 slaves taken, valued at $200 cash each make	<u>$68,200</u>
The whole amounts to:	$428,000

12th [April 1680]. A barque laden with wheat was sent by the admiral, the Christians all escaping in their boat.

13th. Another laden with olive oil with 14 Christians was also sent in by him.

14th. Being informed this morning that one of these Turks' captains (called Mustapha Rais Four-Beards) had presumed to spread His Majesty's Jack-Flag at his ship's bowsprit end; I sent him word, that I must have that flag immediately taken down and sent to my house without more ado, and so it was.

24th. Three of these ships arrived from Troy-Point with timber to forward the ship on the stocks.

27th. Three of these men-of-war departed [for a raid], when the admiral with four others returned from the Levant, where they had been upon the same lawful occasions of robbing.

3rd May. Another of these ships departed for the Gulf of Lepanto with 250 negroes.

13th. This morning sailed a single man-of-war to look for purchase, and at the same time I cashiered my conceited, foolish, impertinent, false, traitorous, base, drunken druggerman, who is called Hassan Agha; who before his voluntarily turning Turk was named Edward Fountain, of a good family in Norfolk as he pretends; a hopeful branch, and a great comfort to his relations!

16th. A squadron consisting of the admiral, vice-admiral, and three other of these men-of-war sailed off in haste for Alexandria where they are to careen, and cruise in those parts this summer, to prevent the dangers from the French, who are hourly expected here with a fleet of ships and galleys to work some mighty achievements against this long threatened place.

21st. The Admiral of Tunis Mustapha Rais Paroslee, my particular friend, attended by a stout merchantman, arrived here from Alexandria bound for Tunis, but hearing that country was as deeply embroiled as ever, they intend to stay here awaiting further news.

22nd. A brigantine of this place went a men-stealing.

24th. The pink *Francis and Benjamin*, Captain John Carter departed for Livorno.

26th. Two stout ships and two great brigantines came into this port from Alexandria bound for Algiers richly laden, besides many Turks and Moors as passengers. They put in here for fear of the Malta galleys.

QUESTIONS TO CONSIDER FOR SECTION III:

Who were the corsairs of Algiers in the late sixteenth century? How did they treat their captives? How did captives describe their captors?

How did North African princes address sea raiding or captive exchange in their correspondence with English monarchs?

Does Mediterranean piracy seem to have become routine by the seventeenth century?

SECTION IV: THE AGE OF DUTCH CORSAIRS

The years between roughly 1600 and 1648, when Spain finally dropped its claims to the United Provinces of the Netherlands, were marked by near-constant pillage. Dutch corsairs, often sponsored by the great trading companies of the day, the United East India Company (VOC) and the West India Company (WIC), hammered away at the now-unified Spanish-Portuguese overseas empire (under Habsburg rule 1580–1640). Although the Dutch often claimed their attacks on Spanish and Portuguese towns and vessels were simply an extension of a justified war for independence, the documents below remind us that such a generalization could conceal an array of actions that from the victims' point of view looked like naked, premeditated, unjustifiable theft. As in the sixteenth century, sea travel and even seaside living were by nature hazardous. Dutch corsairs joined storms, fires, and other "acts of God" on merchants' escape clauses and insurance policies.

DOCUMENT 19

An Encounter with Dutch Pirates in the Philippines (1600)[1]

Dutch corsairs followed Francis Drake to the Pacific hoping to raid Spanish towns and shipping along the west coasts of North and South America and also to attempt capture of a Manila galleon, or "China ship," preferably one leaving Acapulco laden with silver. A privately funded Dutch expedition captained by Olivier van Noort reached the Philippines in December of 1600, where an ambitious crown official based in Manila, Antonio de Morga, decided to go on the attack. Van Noort and his ship Maurice barely escaped. Morga survived by swimming to shore after

1. Source: Antonio de Morga, *Sucesos de las Islas Filipinas*, ed. José Rizal (Paris: Garnier, 1890), 169–171. (Translation Kris Lane.)

his ship, the San Diego, *sank from a well-aimed Dutch cannon-*
ball. The following is how Morga remembered the engagement,
referring to himself in the third person as "the judge."

At the chosen hour both our flagship [*San Diego*] and second-in-command set out in a brief stretch of good weather, sailing throughout the night on the way to Baleitegui. Two outrigger escorts could not follow since the sea was choppy with a fresh nor'easter. They crossed over into the bay, in the shelter of the island. And at daybreak both ships of the fleet found themselves upon the point, descrying to leeward about a league out to sea the two corsair vessels riding at anchor. Soon after, they spotted us, and seeing that we flew the banners of flagship and second-in-command, they weighed anchor and made sail after transferring a boatload of people from the second-in-command to the flagship [the *Maurice*].

Their second-in-command set out to sea while their flagship came about toward our fleet, firing some guns at long range. Our flagship, which could not respond to her since her portholes were shut, tacked to starboard, resolving to overtake the enemy. We came alongside their flagship on the port side and cleared her decks of people, sending aboard a troop of thirty soldiers and sailors. They took control of the stern castle, striking her colors and the standard she had flying from the poop, the white, blue, and orange with the coat-of-arms of Count Maurice. Our men stripped the mainmast and mizzen of all sail and tackle, and they took a large bark they kept stored on the poop deck.

The enemy had retired to the bow, beneath the nets, and seeing two ships upon them with such determination, they sent the judge a request for surrender terms. And as he was responding, the second-in-command, Juan de Alcega, defying his instructions from the day before to come alongside the flagship and assist, decided to give chase to the [enemy's] second-in-command, it seeming to him that this battle was finished and the other corsair was getting away. So he left the two flagships and sailed with all canvas out until he caught up with the other, under command of Lamberto Viezman.

Seeing himself alone but with a better ship and artillery than those of the judge, [the Dutch captain] Olivier van Noort withdrew the request for parley and began to fight again with musket and artillery fire. The combat carried on for more than six hours, each side fighting stubbornly and bitterly, and with deaths on both sides. But the corsair always got the worst of it, with only fifteen men remaining alive, and most of these badly injured, some chopped to pieces. Finally, a fire broke out on the corsair's ship, with flames leaping up above the mizzen and poop, such that the judge, so as not to lose his vessel, took the enemy's colors and his people and returned to his own, pushing off and parting.

But he soon discovered that with the force of so much artillery fire his flagship had opened up around the bows. It was taking on so much water that it would have to be abandoned. The corsair, seeing the struggles of his counterpart, which could no longer pursue him, hurried with the few people that remained to extinguish the fire their ship suffered, and once under control they set off with nothing but the spritsail they had remaining, and despite being destroyed in all parts and devoid of people they reached Borneo and the Sunda Straits, where the corsair was seen so finished off and disheveled that it seemed impossible for him to sail or go on without total loss.

Meanwhile the Spanish flagship, so desperately seeking a remedy for its troubles, found itself without salvation, being alone and so far from land. And thus she began to sink, so quickly that her crew had no time to pull off their armor or grab anything that might have been useful to them. The judge did not abandon ship, although some soldiers took charge of the ship's boat trailing at the stern to save themselves, and they got into it and went off quickly so that no one else would take it from them.

Leaving the ship behind, but holding onto the standard and colors of the enemy, the judge swam for four hours until he arrived at a very small islet, two leagues from there, called Fortuna, where a few others had also saved themselves from the shipwreck, having the will to sustain themselves in the sea. Many others perished and drowned, not having disarmed themselves, suddenly faced with an emergency but too tired from the long battle with the enemy. Those who died on this occasion were fifty persons of all station, among them the most famous.

DOCUMENT 20

Catch as Catch Can: Joris van Speilbergen's Pacific Journal (1615)[2]

Dutch corsairs backed off during the Twelve Years Truce with Spain between 1609 and 1621, but not everyone sought to keep the peace. Another world-encompassing expedition led by Joris van Speilbergen (also spelled "Spilbergen") set out from the Netherlands with five substantial vessels in August 1614. By May the following year Speilbergen was attempting to make alliances with native Chileans, and on July 18 his small fleet got the better of a Spanish armada, or small naval force, one of whose crewmembers was Catalina de Erauso, later famous for her adventures dressed as a male swashbuckler. As the corsairs sailed north, they captured several small vessels, raided a deserted town, and set ashore a few prisoners, possibly including Catalina de Erauso (treated in the next document).

On the 20th [July 1615], the wind being favorable, we passed by [an] island and sailed straight to the harbor [of Callao, port of Lima], where we saw about fourteen vessels of all kinds which carried on trade with Peru, continually going and coming along the coast; for which reason we could not get near them, since it was not deep enough for us so near the land.

We therefore decided to carry out our first intention of anchoring in the roadstead of Callao de Lima, in order to learn whether perchance the Spanish Admiral [the flagship or *almiranta* attacked by Speilbergen's fleet days before near the port of Cañete] might not have escaped, but not finding him there we felt certain that he must have gone down, whereof we were fully assured in Huarmey and Paita, as will be told hereafter.

When we had now come nearer Callao de Lima, our flagship, sailing in advance of the others, cast anchor in nine or ten fathoms, and that close to the shore. But no sooner had he anchored than the enemy, having planted on land a gun firing 36 pound iron shots, and a few other small ones, fired many times upon him, but still without doing him any damage. Our *jagher*, also lying at anchor beside the Admiral, got a shot from

2. Source: Joris van Speilbergen, *The East and West Indian Mirror*, ed. and trans. J. A. J. Villiers (London: Hakluyt Society, 1906), 78–81.

the aforesaid gun right through her, so that she was very near having been sent to the bottom.

Meanwhile, as we saw upon the shore a large number of troops, amongst whom, as we afterwards learnt, was the viceroy himself, escorted by eight companies of horse and 4,000 men on foot; as we further heard that the ships lying along the shore had also troops and the necessary means of defense on board; and as, moreover, we were, by reason of the land-firing, like to lose our masts or rigging, which might have retarded our voyage: it was, therefore, after mature deliberation, resolved by the Admiral and all the officers, since no advantage was to be gained here, to retire a mile or two, which was immediately done, as appears from the minutes of the general council. Also, that we cast anchor at the entrance to the harbor of Callao de Lima, where we lay until the 25th of this month of July, meanwhile making every effort to catch some of their ships; but this was in vain, since the said vessels, going and coming along the shore, sailed more rapidly than ours, so that we gained no advantage, except that our boats captured and brought to the fleet a small vessel that was scarcely of any value.

On the 26th, we once more set sail to continue our voyage, hugging the shore as closely as possible until the afternoon, when we saw a small vessel quite near the land, to capture which our Admiral sent out three well-manned boats, our fleet not waiting for these but proceeding on its course until evening, when we cast anchor in 15 fathoms. This having been done, our boats returned, bringing with them the aforesaid little vessel, which was laden with salt and about 80 tons of syrup, this being divided amongst us in equal shares.

On the approach of our men, the Spaniards on the vessel had fled ashore, taking with them as much as they had been able to carry. The Admiral, deciding to keep this vessel with our fleet, placed upon her a crew consisting of a few sailors, with Jan de Wit as captain.

On the 27th, we once more set sail, the wind being northwest by north, with fine weather. On the 28th, we reached the roadstead of Huarmey, situated in the latitude of 10 degrees south of the [Equatorial] Line. This town of Huarmey is very fine and pleasant, and has a very large and well-situated harbor, in which many ships can lie. There is also a constant pool of fresh water, from which we got our supply.

On first arriving, the Admiral sent a troop of soldiers ashore, but they found only empty dwellings since the inhabitants, being informed of our coming, had fled to the woods, so that our men got little booty.

As long as we lay here the Admiral repeatedly sent ashore Jan Baptista, skipper of the little vessel we had captured the day before the battle, in order to examine all the commodities and obtain some supply of provisions. But after the aforesaid had examined everything he found in the end only some oranges and other fruits. The sailors also found in the houses some fowls, pigs, and meal. A faithful and discreet man was also sent out to obtain tidings of Don Rodrigo and his fleet, and at last he learnt with certainty that both the King's galleons had gone down, and that not a single individual had been saved.

On the 3rd of August, the Admiral released and set ashore some Spanish prisoners, who expressed much gratitude to him for this favor.

DOCUMENT 21

Catch and Release? Catalina de Erauso and the Dutch Corsairs (1615)[3]

Born in Spain's Basque Country around 1590, Catalina de Erauso fled the convent as an adolescent dressed as a boy. She made her way to Seville, and then to the Americas as a page. After a scrape with Dutch corsairs in the Caribbean near Venezuela's Punta de Araya, Erauso made it to Peru, where she became known as an able sword fighter. In her autobiography, written about 1625, Erauso recounts her experience as a prisoner of Joris van Speilbergen. Her memory of the sea battle off Cañete seems a bit confused, but the story of being put ashore near Paita seems to be corroborated by the Dutch account quoted above. As with the tales of her Spanish contemporary in the Mediterranean, Alonso de Contreras, Catalina de Erauso's autobiography has enough elements of the picaresque novel to make it a winning source, but one to be approached with extreme caution.

I arrived in Lima in the days when Don Juan de Mendoza y Luna, the Marquis of Montes Claros, was the viceroy of Peru. The Dutch were

---

3. Source: Catalina de Erauso, *Lieutenant Nun: Memoir of a Basque Transvestite in the New World*, trans. Michele and Gabriel Stepto (Boston: Beacon Press, 1996), 52–53.

laying siege to Lima with eight warships that had been stationed off the coast, and the city was armed to the teeth. We went out to meet them from the port of Callao in five ships, and for a long time it went well for us, but then the Dutch began hammering away at our flagship and in the end she heaved over and only three of us managed to escape— me, a barefoot Franciscan friar, and a soldier—paddling around until the enemy ship took us up. The Dutch treated us like dirt, jeering and scoffing. All the others who had been on the flagship had drowned. Four ships remained under General Don Rodrigo de Mendoza, and when they got back to Callao the next morning at least 900 men were reckoned as missing, myself included, because I'd been on the flagship.

For 26 days I was in enemy hands, thinking they meant to deal with me by carting me off to Holland. But in the end they flung me and my two companions out on the Paita coast, a good hundred leagues from Lima, and after several days and no end of trouble a good man took pity on our naked state, gave us some clothes and gear and pointed us back in the direction of Lima, and we finally made it back.

DOCUMENT 22

Declaration of Pedro Angola, Captured by the Dutch at Puerto Rico (1626)[4]

After the expiration of the Twelve Years Truce in 1621, Dutch corsair activity exploded worldwide. No ship flying Spanish or Portuguese colors was safe in any seas, least of all in the Caribbean, an old and favored hunting ground rich in silver, gold, precious stones, and human captives. A Dutch attack on San Juan, Puerto Rico, in September of 1625 is still remembered as a very close call—a near loss. Among those captured by the Dutch in this attack were a number of enslaved Africans, some of whom later escaped to provide Spanish officials with intelligence on Dutch designs in sworn testimony. Pedro Angola was interviewed on the pearling island of Margarita, off the coast of Venezuela. As was standard at the time, he refers to the Dutch as Flemings.

4. Source: Archivo General de Indias, Santo Domingo 180, ramo 3, no. 1, fols. 1–2. (Translation Kris Lane.)

Declaration of Pedro Angola

In the city of Asunción on this island of Margarita, 1st of March, 1626, the lord Don Andrés Rodríguez de Villegas, governor of this island for Your Majesty . . . made to appear before him the said black man, from whom was received sworn testimony as he is a Christian and half-latinized, as he said he was, and he did so well and willingly; and having been sworn in and questioned according to the prepared inquiry, he said:

That he is called Pedro, of the Angola nation, from the island of Puerto Rico, and his first master was a Mr. So-and-so Morcelo, and he was given as bridewealth to Gerónimo de Ahuero, who married one of Morcelo's daughters.

And that when the Flemings took the said city of San Juan de Puerto Rico, after they got inside and placed a ship near the bridge, a black slave of the king, known as Shark, and by name Francisco, along with some other blacks, how many this deponent does not know except that there were many. Shark made himself captain and took them to the Flemish ship, and this deponent with them along with four others belonging to his master, called "Crab," "Boss Pedro," "Little Juan," and "Pablo," but most of the other blacks were taken at Toa and they were put in irons on the [Dutch] ships.

And he saw them take a white man in the mouth of Toa; he does not know his name but he was on the general's ship.

And that many Flemings died, killed in Puerto Rico.

And the Flemings burned many ships by the tile oven laded with ginger and sugar; and one Flemish ship remained in Puerto Rico having run aground in front of the governor's house; and the Flemish abandoned it and left it there; and all the other ships, after leaving Puerto Rico, went to water at Guadianilla, where they also killed people; and also after leaving Puerto Rico they sent two ships to Holland with sugar, ginger, and wine; and they went to request more ships from their king to come to Puerto Rico again to take the fortress, since now they had few people; and they would rendezvous in the land of the Caribs, among the Windward Islands, and they took two frigates outside Puerto Rico in the mouth of Bayamón, and another two vessels were taken at sea with wines, and these ships were burned.

He was asked what these Flemings did after taking Puerto Rico and taking on water: he said they went out to sea and made landfall in a place out there with no people, and there they dropped anchor and remained a few days; then they sailed to Santo Domingo, where they passed by the port and fired their guns, but they put no one ashore; and they went to Carib lands, where they rendezvoused with six ships of their own that had arrived from Angola, already waiting there; and they remained there awaiting other companions that had also gone to Angola, whereas the general [of the Puerto Rico raiders] left with his ships to capture the fortress at Margarita . . .

He was asked how he managed to get ashore from these ships, if he was sent as a spy and how many others were sent out with him to swim: he said that he fled from the ship on which he came on his own, having been left alone to swab the decks, all his companions having gone back to Holland sent from Puerto Rico, and seeing himself alone he fled, as he did not know the Flemish language and they did not speak with him, and he swam away after they had gone to sleep, he climbing out through one of the gun ports, and he stayed in the bush all night hiding until daylight, and he found a trail and encountered an Indian who wanted to shoot him with an arrow, and this deponent asked why he wanted to shoot him, offering to be bound instead, and the Indian bound him and handed him over to the whites who took him to the governor.

DOCUMENT 23

Spanish Notice of Diego de los Reyes
a.k.a. Diego el Mulato (1635)[5]

European renegades were numerous among the Barbary corsairs. In the Caribbean a few people of African descent seem also to have turned to piracy, joining others to seek revenge, glory, or simply wealth in a way not possible under Spanish rule. The story of Diego de los Reyes, better known as Diego el Mulato, appears to have been one such example. He had initially been the master of a turtling barque that was seized by Dutch raiders off Cuba in 1632. After a spell in the Netherlands, where he married the

---

5. Source: Archivo General de Indias, Patronato 273, ramo 3, fols. 22–23. (Translation Kris Lane.)

daughter of a mapmaker, he returned to the New World and was active pillaging Spanish vessels all over the Caribbean. The following letter, penned by the governor and captain-general of Cuba, describes encounters with the pirate at a time when he was barely known, which explains the erroneous birthplace.

My Lord:

Friday, April 13, at ten at night, there entered into the port of Havana a launch of the sort that trades along these coasts, whose skipper is Francisco Galindo, and in which came another skipper of a small vessel, Cristobal de Cañete, a mate of the same trade, with their companions.

And according to the declarations taken from both skippers it appeared that while coming from the Tortugas on a Saturday, Cañete, at oars and within sight of this port, six leagues out to sea, spied a ship that lay closer to the port, and seeing that it was going to enter, he backed off. And the ship, having gone farther down, came after the small vessel with seventeen sails out, and she turned around and fled toward the Florida coast, but seeing that it was gaining on her she struck sail at noon. They engaged her at one in the afternoon, firing a cannon to drive off a launch, and there came aboard the Dutch pirate Peg-leg [Cornelis Jol], with another eighteen men, and putting the people aboard his ship, seeing that the small vessel carried only turtles, he scuttled her.

And on Wednesday, April 11, when the ship was off Cayo de Piedras, Francisco Galindo was anchored at night, loading turtles from the old canal, and up came the enemies in their launch and overpowered Galindo, taking him and his companions to the ship, where they were held until afternoon the next day, Thursday, April 12, when they were returned to their own launch, along with Cañete and his companions, and from there they took off, the ship sailing toward this port [of Havana].

They say the ship is about 150 tons, very long and plain, good to sail in as little as 12 palms of water, with 70 Dutchmen and among them some Italians. She had 18 artillery pieces and plenty of munitions and supplies. They said they had left Holland some three months earlier along with another five ships headed for these parts, but they did not say where. And in this ship they had only a few days before they put in at the port of [Santiago de] Cuba, where they searched for copper as well as prize ships, if they could find them. They captured a frigate in port loaded for Cartagena, and taking out of it the hides, tallow, and lard it carried they scuttled it. And they set fire to another four frigates there, all empty. They said they would not have done this had the governor not refused to ransom them.

They came with orders to burn or scuttle all ships taken, but they held two vessels in reserve, and they would remain about this port until they had taken good prizes in silver, cochineal, and silks to take back to Holland.

What follows is the report from the attack on Santiago de Cuba, followed by this: And they said that some fifteen days back they left the island of Curaçao, where they had arrived on orders from Holland, and that there remained there 900 men, fortifying themselves with the intention of carrying on, their daily sustenance supplied from home; and they brought with them as chief pilot, a mulatto called Diego de los Reyes, native of Seville, married in Holland, and they went to the port of [Santiago de] Cuba searching for copper, and having done what was described above they took two ships that arrived from the New Spain fleet and sailed off, threatening to return to the port with greater force.

Havana, May 25, 1635
Don Francisco Riaño y Gamboa

DOCUMENT 24

The English-American Meets Diego el Mulato (1637)[6]

Between 1625 and 1637 the Dominican friar Thomas Gage served as a missionary in Guatemala. On his way back to his native England, Gage—styled "the English-American" in his travel account—visited Honduras, Nicaragua, and Costa Rica, and then took a Spanish vessel to Cartagena. At sea the vessel was seized and looted by freebooters. In Cartagena's notorious prison, Gage ministered to a number of captured pirates before he left for good. He later converted to Protestantism and became a prominent advocate of Oliver Cromwell's Western Design, a plan to upset Spanish control of the Caribbean. In his account of the New World, published in 1648 and reprinted several times,

---

6. Source: Thomas Gage, *The English-American, His Travail by Sea and Land: or, A New Survey of the West-Indies* (London: Richard Cotes, 1648), 188–90.

Gage described his encounter with the pirate gang led by Diego el Mulato.

We came in so good a time to the River Suerre that we stayed there but three days in a Spanish farm near unto it, and departed. The master of the frigate was exceedingly glad of our company, and offered to carry me for nothing, but for my prayers to God for him, and for a safe passage, which we hoped would not be above three or four days' sailing. What he carried was nothing but some honey, hides, bacon, meal, and fowls. The greatest danger he told us of was the setting out from the river (which runs in some places with a very strong stream, is shallow and full of rocks in other places) till we come forth to the main sea.

Whither we got out safely and had not sailed on above twenty leagues when we discovered two ships making toward us; our hearts began to quake, and the master himself of the frigate we perceived was not without fear, who suspected that they were English, or Holland ships. We had no guns nor weapons to fight with, save only four or five muskets and half a dozen swords. We thought the wings of our nimble frigate might be our best comfort, and flying away our chiefest safety. But this comfort soon began to fail us, and our best safety was turned to near approaching danger; for before we could fly on five leagues toward Portobelo, we could from our top mast easily perceive the two ships to be Hollanders, and too nimble for our little vessel, which presently one of them (which being a man-of-war was too much and too strong for our weakness) fetched up, and with a thundering message made us strike sail. Without any fighting we durst not but yield, hoping for better mercy.

But Oh, what sad thoughts did here run to and fro my dejected heart, which was struck down lower than our sail! How did I sometimes look upon death's frighting visage! But if again I should comfort and encourage myself against this fear of death; how then did I begin to see an end of all my hopes of ever more returning to my wished and desired country! How did I see that my treasure of pearls, precious stones, pieces of eight, and golden pistoles, which by singing I had got in twelve years' space, now within one half hour ready to be lost with weeping, and become a sure prey to those who with as much ease as I got them, and with laughing, were ready to spoil me of all that with the sound of flutes, waits, and organs I had so long been hoarding up! Now I saw I must forcedly and feignedly offer up to a Hollander what superstitious, yea also forced and feigned, offerings of Indians to their saints of Mixco, Pinola, Amatitlan, and Petapa had for a while enriched me.

My further thoughts were soon interrupted by the Hollanders who came aboard our frigate with more speed than we desired. Though their swords, muskets, and pistols did not a little terrify, yet we were somewhat comforted when we understood who was their chief captain and commander, and hoped for more mercy from him, who had been born and brought up amongst Spaniards, than from the Hollanders, who as they were little bound unto the Spanish nation for mercy, so did we expect little from them.

The captain of this Holland ship which took us was a mulatto born and bred in Havana, whose mother I saw and spoke with afterwards that same year, when the galleons struck into that port to expect there the rest that were to come from Veracruz. This mulatto, for some wrongs which had been offered unto him from some commanding Spaniards in Havana, ventured himself desperately in a boat out to the sea, where were some Holland ships waiting for a prize, and with God's help getting unto them, yielded himself to their mercy, which he esteemed far better than that of his own countrymen, promising to serve them faithfully against his own nation, which had most injuriously and wrongfully abused, yea and (I was afterwards informed) whipped him in Havana.

This mulatto proved so true and faithful in his good services unto the Hollanders that they esteemed much of him, married him to one of their nation, and made him captain of a ship under that brave and gallant Hollander whom the Spaniards then so much feared, and named Pie de Palo, or Peg-leg. This famous mulatto it was that with his sea soldiers boarded our frigate, in which he had found little worth his labor had it not been for the Indians' offerings which I carried with me, of which I lost that day the worth of 4,000 patacones or pieces of eight in pearls and precious stones, and near 3,000 more in money. The other Spaniards lost some hundreds apiece, which was so rich a prize that it made the Hollanders' stomach loath the rest of our gross provision of bacon, meal, and fowls, and our money tasted sweeter to them than the honey which our frigate also afforded them.

Other things I had (as a quilt to lie on, some books, and laminas, which are pictures in brass, and clothes) which I begged of that noble captain the mulatto, who considering my orders and calling, gave me them freely and wished me to be patient, saying that he could do no otherwise than he did with my money and pearls, and using that common proverb at sea:

'Hoy por mi, mañana por ti,' today fortune hath been for me, tomorrow it may be for thee.

I had some comfort left in a few pistoles, some single, some double, which I had sewed up in my quilt (which the captain restored unto me, saying it was the bed I lay in) and in the doublet which I had at that present, which mounted to almost a thousand crowns, and in their searching was not found out. After the captain and soldiers had well viewed their prize, they thought of refreshing their stomachs with some of our provision; the good captain made a stately dinner in our frigate and invited me unto it, and knowing that I was going toward Havana, besides many other brindis or healths, he drank one unto his mother, desiring me to see her and to remember him unto her, and that how for her sake he had used me well and courteously in what he could; and further at table he said that for my sake he would give us our frigate that we might return again to land, and that I might find out from thence some safer way and means to get to Portobelo, and to continue on my journey unto Spain.

After dinner I conferred with the captain alone, and told him that I was no Spaniard, but an Englishman born, shewing him the license which I had from Rome to go to England, and that therefore I hoped, not being of an enemy nation to the Hollanders, he would restore unto me what goods were mine. But all this was of little consequence with him, who had already taken possession of mine and all other goods in the ship: he told me I must suffer with those amongst whom I was found, and that I might as well claim all the goods in my ship for mine. I desired him then to carry me along with him to Holland, that from thence I might get to England, which he also refused to do, telling me that he went about from one place to another and knew not when he should go to Holland, and that he was daily ready to fight with any Spanish ship, and if he should fight with the Spaniards whilst I was in his ship, his soldiers in their hot blood might be ready to do me a mischief, thinking I would do them harm if in fight they should be taken by the Spaniards. With these his answers I saw there was no hope of getting again what now was lost, therefore (as before) I commended myself again to God's providence and protection.

The soldiers and mariners of the Holland ship made haste that afternoon to unlade the goods of our frigate into their man-of-war, which took them up that and the part of the next day, whilst we as prisoners were wafting up and down the sea with them. And whereas we thought our money had satisfied them enough and to the full, we found the next day that they had also a stomach to our fowls and bacon, and wanted our meal to make them bread, and our honey to sweeten their mouths, and our hides for shoes and boots, all which they took away, leaving me my quilt, books, and brass pictures, and to the master of the frigate some small provision, as much as might carry us to land, which was not far off, and thus they took their leaves of us, thanking us for their good entertainment.

Questions to consider for Section IV:

What drove the Dutch corsairs to the Pacific? What did they find?

What were the special challenges of these long-distance raids?

What enabled the rise of corsairs like the renegade Diego el Mulato?

What else may one learn from captives of the Dutch?

SECTION V: THE BUCCANEERS

In contrast to previous generations of pirates, the buccaneers who emerged in the 1630s were based in the Caribbean. Tortuga, a small island off the northwest coast of Hispaniola, served as their first base. Access to supplies and colonial markets enabled freebooters to embark on voyages that lasted many months, sometimes years. In the course of such ventures some gangs not only seized vessels at sea, they also advanced deep into Spanish territory. For many years France, the Netherlands, and England tolerated opportunistic marauding bands or directly supported them by issuing commissions that legitimized pillage. The number of assaults on Spanish targets increased dramatically after the English conquest of Jamaica in 1655. In the late 1660s, at the height of raiding, more than 1,500 freebooters were based in Port Royal, many of whom had no source of income other than plunder. The buccaneers weakened Spain's grip on the New World while simultaneouly providing their respective colonies with much-needed capital before plantations could generate enormous profits. When English authorities slowly began to turn against rogue privateers in the 1670s, the southwest coast of Hispaniola, particularly Petit-Goâve and Cape Tiburon, served as bases for numerous raiders.

DOCUMENT 25

Jean de Laon on the Early Buccaneers (1654)[1]

In an ill-advised attempt to curb connections to Dutch contraband traders, the Spanish governor forced the inhabitants of Hispaniola's northern and western littoral in 1605 and 1606 to abandon their settlements. In the following years Frenchmen infiltrated this region and established a colony on Tortuga. While the earliest settlers cut dyewood and established tobacco plantations, others undertook forays deeper into Hispaniola and hunted

1. Source: Jean de Laon, *Relation du voyage des François fait au Cap de Nord en Amérique* (Paris: Edme Pepingué, 1654), 156–57. (Translation Arne Bialuschewski.)

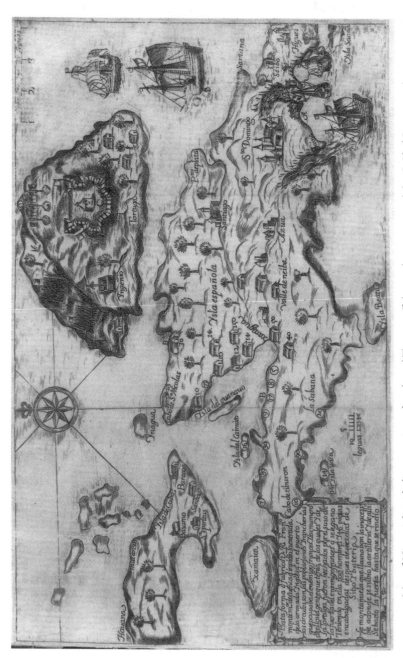

Map of Hispaniola with disproportionately enlarged Tortuga off the northwest coast and the Gulf of Saragua in the west. Cape of the Plateforme is located on the northern peninsula and Gonaïves in the bay just southeast of it. Cape Tiburon is at the end of the southwestern peninsula. John Carter Brown Library at Brown University.

hogs, goats, cattle, and also horses that had turned feral after the Spaniards had left. Hides were greatly sought after in Europe and therefore quite valuable. This account of the frontiersmen was written by a royal engineer and infantry captain who described his voyage from Guyana back to France. He provides a rare contemporary view of these social outcasts before raiding became their main activity.

On the 14th of February [1653] finding ourselves before the wind from Tortuga, by improvidence of our commander, who had gone without taking a look at the yards, we resolved to put into the Gulf of Saragua in Santo Domingo, to take in water and to replenish our victuals, but we were becalmed near the Cape of the Plateforme. This lasted until Sunday the 23rd when we anchored in Gonaïves, having been driven there by a westerly wind they call Aquilon. There the buccaneers who were ashore shot three volleys of musketry, for there were three crews. We answered them with three rounds of cannon fire, and since we needed their hunting, we were obliged to shower them with honors. Then a price was agreed with them for providing us with meat while we would take in our water.

It is necessary to explain to the curious reader what the term buccaneer means. These are for the most part the most debauched people who do not know what it is like to exercise acts of religion. They live almost year round in the woods, eating the flesh of cattle and pigs without bread. They produce a lot of hides that are much larger and stronger than ours in France, and when they have amassed a quantity, they send them to France to make a lot of money, and then they return to resume their life in the wilderness.

DOCUMENT 26

A Commission and Instructions for Jamaican Privateers (1662)[2]

After the conquest of 1655 naval vessels defended Jamaica for a while, but they were soon ordered back to England. Beginning in

---

2. Source: The National Archives, High Court of Admiralty 49/59, fols. 91–92.

1659 a shift occurred and privateers increasingly assaulted Span-
ish shipping and port towns. Besides strategic motives, mate-
rial gain was the driving force behind these ventures. Jamaican
governors issued numerous commissions to attack and plunder
Spanish holdings all over the Caribbean, even in periods when
there was no war in Europe. The justification, along with detailed
instructions for the commander of an armed vessel, is outlined in
the following commission that survives among Jamaica's earliest
admiralty records.

Thomas, Lord Windsor, Peer of the Realm of England, Lord Lieutenant of the County of Worcester, and of the city and county of the same,
Governor of Jamaica and islands thereto adjacent, Commander-in-Chief
there of all the forces by sea and land, and Vice-Admiral to His Royal
Highness the Duke of York in the American Seas, to George Brimacam,
greetings.

Whereas His most sacred Majesty having taken into his serious
consideration, and apprehending that divers well-affected people of
his Kingdom of England and other his dominions and territories have
sustained great wrongs, losses and damages as well at sea in their ships,
goods, wares, and merchandises, being pillaged, spoiled, surprised,
and taken by the ships and subjects of the King of Spain as by divers
unlawful seizures, wrongs, and violences used against both their persons
and goods in several ports and on shore in his dominions in America and
the Spanish governor refusing and utterly revoking all commerce and
trade contrary to justice and all manner of civil correspondence between
prince and prince and to the lawful nations to the manifest prejudice
and destruction to the trade, commerce and navigation of the King, my
Master's subjects.

Therefore know ye that by virtue of authority derived from His most
excellent Majesty and His Royal Highness the Duke of York, that I do
thereby give and grant unto you, the said George Brimacam, the command of the good ship or frigate called the *Fortune*, a private man-of-war,
which he (the said George Brimacam) has armed in a warlike manner, and
armed, equipped and furnished to all intents and purposes whatsoever.

And further know ye that by authority thereof, I do license and autho-
rise the said Captain George Brimacam to set forth to sea the said ship
the *Fortune* and therewith to apprehend, take, seize or surprise, or by
force of arms to set upon, take and apprehend any of the ships, goods

wares and merchandises of the said King of Spain, or any of his subjects whatsoever, upon the high land, open seas, or any of ports or harbors within the dominions and territories of the said King of Spain in America, or any other person without license first obtained carrying to them men, ammunitions or provisions; and the same ships, goods, wares and merchandises so taken, do without delay, or any prisoner whatsoever, bring into the harbour of Point Cagway within this island of Jamaica without breach of bulk or embezzlement of any pays, bills of lading, charter parties, cockets, or other documents and writings whatsoever which may concern the said prize, and shall not dispose or alter the property thereof until the same be legally adjudged in the Court of Admiralty here established in Jamaica, the tenths and fifteenths of all such prizes, or the full value thereof, first duly taken out and paid to such persons as shall be by me nominated and appointed to the use of the King, my Master, or His Royal Highness the Duke of York.

And that it shall and may be lawful for any subject of the King, my Master, whatsoever either in his own person to serve or otherwise to bear charge and adventure or in any sort further, or to set forward the said enterprise by virtue of these presents, and that it shall and may be lawful for all persons whatsoever, being subjects of the King, my Master, or any others, to contract, bargain for or buy the said ship or ship's goods, wares and merchandises whatsoever perishable or other lawful cause seeming fit to the judge of the said Court of Admiralty without any danger, hindrance, loss, trouble or molestation whatsoever provided always, and it is the true intent and meaning of these presents that you neither do permit or suffer to be done any violence or injury to the ships, goods, wares, and merchandises presently belonging to the subjects of any prince or state in league or amity with the King, my Master, to whose aid and assistance I recommend you.

My execution of this commission whereof you shall enjoy the benefit and the same continue in full force and virtue for the space of ten months next ensuing the date hereof, unless I shall for just reasons in the meantime think fit to revoke the same, whereof you shall have timely notice.

Passed and registered in the said Court of Admiralty, and given under my hand, at Point Cagway, the 18th day of September in the fourteenth year of the reign of Our Sovereign Lord Charles the Second, by the Grace of God, King of England, Scotland, France and Ireland, Defender of the Faith, etc., and Lord of Jamaica, and in the year of Our Lord 1662.

Windsor

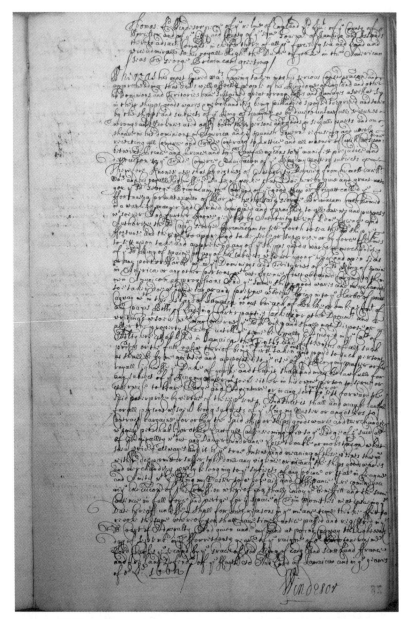

Lord Windsor's commission for George Brimacam. The National Archives.

Instructions which are to be observed, performed, fulfilled and kept by George Brimacam, commander of the frigate called the *Fortune*.

1. You shall give all due respect and obedience to such petitions as His Royal Highness or myself shall give to any vessel at sea, and shall not presume in any degree to violate or infringe the same.

2. Upon taking any ship or vessel you shall forthwith cause an inventory to be taken of all bills of lading and other goods omitted out of such bills without breaking of bulk, and you shall deliver a copy of the inventory signed by yourself and the chief officers of your ship to the judge of Admiralty at Jamaica, and you shall, as soon as you are possessed of any such ship, seal up decks and not suffer any bulk to be broken until adjudication be first obtained.

3. Upon taking any vessel you shall immediately cause the master and other officers of the said ship so taken to be examined touching the design of their voyage, from whence they came and whither they are bound, with such other questions as you shall think fit to demand, which examination shall be reduced into writing and delivered to the judge of the Court of Admiralty here established, and if the said prize seem doubtful, then you shall keep the said master and other officers so taken till they be personally all examined by the said judge if he sees cause.

4. Upon your going on shore in any place whatsoever after the taking of a prize, or upon your arrival and coming to anchor in the harbor of Point Cagway in Jamaica, you shall neither suffer seaman or soldier, or any other person whatsoever either of your own ship or belonging to the prize, to come on shore before they be searched and examined what they carry with them.

5. Upon bringing in a prize into the harbor of Point Cagway in Jamaica, and adjudication thereupon obtained, the fifteenths due unto His Majesty's and the tenths due unto His Royal Highness the Duke of York and the just fees of the court shall be first deducted and paid before any particular division be made between owners, victuallers and seamen.

6. You shall not suffer any officer, seaman or soldier whatsoever embezzle, cancel or throw over board any writing whatsoever found in any ship and to break open any packets before they be brought to you, and you shall cause all the said writings so taken to be delivered to the said judge.

7. You shall not presume to take any commission from any other prince, and if you shall take any such commission I do hereby declare that, from that time the commission you have received from me, stands revoked and is determined.

Given under my hand at Point Cagway, the 18th day of September, in the year of Our Lord 1662,
Windsor

DOCUMENT 27

Buccaneers Describe a Raiding Voyage in Central America (1665)[3]

In November 1664 a group of about 140 buccaneers left Jamaica for a lengthy raiding expedition along the Caribbean coast of the Spanish empire. This gang was led by John Morris, Jacob Fackman, and the Dutchman David Maarten. During the voyage Henry Morgan emerged as one of the commanders, presumably based on his able leadership or other accomplishments. Perhaps more importantly, the men learned that they did not have to fear Spanish defenses, and alliances with native groups enabled them to advance deep into the interior of Central America. This highly successful venture served as a model for a series of further raids on prosperous targets that were located not on the shore but far inland where colonial authorities were unprepared to confront heavily armed raiders. The following account provides a detailed description of the strategy and proceedings of the attackers.

The several examinations of Captain John Morris, Captain [Jacob] Fackman and Captain Henry Morgan as it was by them severally told to Sir Thomas Modyford, Baronet, Governor of Jamaica, and the 20th day of September 1665 composed into one narrative.

The examinants say that, having been 22 months out and knowing nothing of the cessation between the King and the Spaniard, they did their best according to their commission from the Lord Windsor to prey upon that nation. And that, about the month of January last, going by the River of Tabasco, which lies in the [Gulf] of Mexico, they took some Indians, who promised to guide them to the town of Villahermosa, to which place

---

3. Source: The National Archives, Colonial Office 1/20, fols. 38–39.

they went 300 miles about that they might not be discovered, and coming upon them in the morning with 107 men they took their fort and guns, wherein was 11 guns, and there took 300 prisoners, and stayed there 24 hours, and calling out the choicest of the prisoners to secure themselves, they went down to the river's mouth and found their ships, which they left there, missing, being taken (as they after understood) by a small Spanish fleet. About ten days after they discovered the Spaniards with their own ships and 300 men on them coming upon them. At first sight of them they cast up a small work on a point of land and planted five great guns, which they had brought from the town. The Spaniards sent a man with a flag and tendered them quarter. They told them they were Englishmen and for the honor of their country did scorn quarter. Whereupon the enemy landed 150 men and with the rest bore up near them in their ships. When they were within shot they fired at them and shot them through and through in several places, and at the same time, their land forces came upon them, but by God's help they beat them both by sea and land without the loss of a man.

After which they released their prisoners and fitted two barques and four canoes and endeavored to turn to windward, and they landed at River Lagartos and took the town with 30 men, but as they drew up in the town, the enemy fired a volley on them from a breastwork, which the Indians told them not of, where was 30 men. They killed four of them. Whereupon they stormed it in the smoke and killed 15 men and took the other 15 Spaniards prisoners. And taking what they wanted, they went aboard and crossed the Bay of Honduras and came to the Island of Roatán and there watered. And sailing for the Mosquitoes, they saw a vessel riding at Trujillo road and took it, and then landed and took the town.

And from thence they came to the Musketoes, which country as also Cape Gracias a Dios on the main right against it are inhabited with Indians that stand upon their guard against the Spaniard and are good friends to the English. From thence, taking nine Indians who willingly went with them, they came to Monkey Bay and there cast anchor near the River [San Juan], where having fitted their canoes, they sent two before up the river to take the lookout, who spied them and fled. However, they went on and in three days they arrived at the lower fall, being 30 leagues up. In 24 hours after they came to the second fall, which was five leagues, where the current ran as fast against them as any tide in England. Next day by noon they came to the last fall, which was two leagues farther, where begun the entrance into a fair lagune or lake, judged to be 50 leagues in

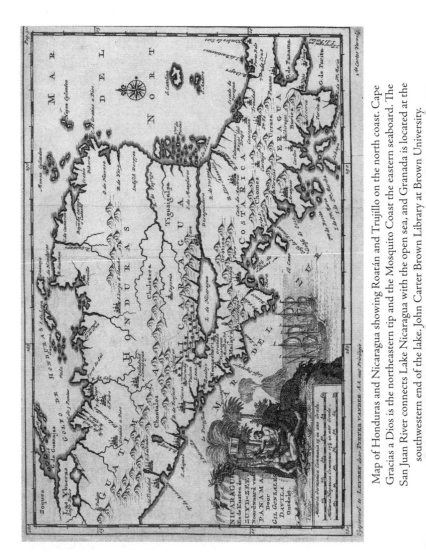

Map of Honduras and Nicaragua showing Roatán and Trujillo on the north coast. Cape Gracias a Dios is the northeastern tip and the Mosquito Coast the eastern seaboard. The San Juan River connects Lake Nicaragua with the open sea, and Granada is located at the southwestern end of the lake. John Carter Brown Library at Brown University.

length and three in breadth, good, wholesome and sweet water, and full of excellent fish of several sorts, all the banks full of brave pastures and savannas covered with cattle and horses, where they had at their return as good beef and mutton as any in England.

This lake is full of small keys and islands, under which they hid themselves all the day and rowed all night to prevent their being discovered. The fifth night after they entered this lagoon by advice of their Indian guide, they landed about two of the clock in the morning, one mile from the city of Granada, and so marched undescried into the middle of the city and suddenly fired a volley of small shot, forthwith seizing and overturning 18 great guns, which they found in the parade place, and took the sergeant major's house, where (our Indian informed them) was all the firearms and ammunition. And having secured in the church 300 of their best men prisoners, abundance of which were churchmen, they fell to plundering and kept the town 16 hours. And then putting their plunder aboard, they discharged the prisoners and sunk all the boats they had no use for and so came away.

This town is twice bigger than Portsmouth. There are seven churches and a very fair cathedral besides divers colleges and monasteries, all built with free stone and so are most of their houses. And they have six camps of foot and horse, besides Indians and slaves. Abundance of which Indians there came to them about 1,000, which plundered as fast as they and would have killed our prisoners, especially the churchmen. They imagined the English would have stayed with them and kept the place. But when they found they would return home, they requested them to come again and told them in the meantime they would go up into the mountains and secure themselves. One with his wife and children [and] three or four more young men came away with them and are in Maarten's vessel, which put into Tortuga, fearing his entertainment here, he being a Dutchman.

Divers of their prisoners in gratitude of their civil usage went down the lagoon with them and entertained them at their several stantions, where was abundance of cattle and good wheat, which made as good bread as ever was eaten. About the end of the lagoon, they took a ship of a 100 tons laden with cables, rigging, tallow, brazil wood, pitch, tar, hemp and flax, which is all produced plentifully in this place. They took also an island in this lagoon at the south end of it called Lida, as big as Barbados, with a fine neat town on it, which they plundered and so came away to their ships.

DOCUMENT 28

Victims Describe the Same Attack on Granada, Nicaragua (1665)[4]

A few months after the raid on Granada—one of the most prosperous and important towns in Central America—the Spanish authorities carried out their own investigation. A fragment of a partly illegible manuscript containing the testimonies of a number of witnesses, specifically their answers to six questions, survives in the colonial archives in Guatemala. This document not only provides a unique insight into the actions of the raiders from the victims' perspective, but also sheds further light on the weaknesses of the Spanish defenses as well as the role that native people played in the pillage.

Witness Juan Gonzáles de Sá

In the city of Granada, Province of Nicaragua, on September 7, 1665, his mercy, the Field Marshal Don Juan Fernández de Salinas y Cerda, knight of the Order of Calatrava, governor of Costa Rica and judge in this inquiry, so as to ascertain the truth of its contents, he made appear before him Juan Gonzáles de Sá, householder of this city, and ordered him sworn in according to law, which the abovesaid did, promising to tell the truth, and in response to the list of questions he said the following:

First. To the first question he said he had heard news of the invasion of this city by Captain David [Maarten] and other enemies that arrived with him since he was one of those robbed and made prisoner, and he also knows the governor, Don Diego de Castro, and the rest of the householders of this city, and thus he responded. As for the general [questions] required by law, he said he did not think any of them touched upon him and if at some point in his testimony he thought they did he would say so and he is above 52 years of age and so he responded.

Second. On the second question he said he knew nothing since he has been absent from this city for some time and thus he responded.

---

4. Source: Archivo General de Centro América, A1 (Guatemala), leg. 4681, exp. 40319, fols. 50–51. (Translation Kris Lane.)

Third. On the third question he said that on the occasion of the present entry of the enemy it was not more than a year ago by order of the judge and governor of this city that there be no sentinels posted on the San Juan River as used to be done in time of [war] and thus he responded.

Fourth. To the fourth question he said that what he knows of this question is that some days before the invasion of this city when this witness was exiting the house he lives in very early one morning he encountered Francisco Pérez de Zárate, householder of this city, who told this witness that news had arrived that the enemy had taken the frigate of Don Francisco Velasco which was in the San Juan River preparing to sail to Portobelo, and thus he responded. And he said that in the same way a little less than a year ago the enemy captured in the same river the frigate of Don Pedro de Ocón, field marshal in this city, and they took off with it, and thus things have always been in this city and he would have done the same, and thus he responded.

Fifth. To the fifth question he said he did not know although when the enemy invaded this city they had not prepared and set a defense force nor does he know if any orders were given to do so, and thus he responded.

Sixth. To the sixth question he said that what he knows is that the night following the day, the 30th of June, around one or two in the morning, this witness being at home in bed, and because [the house] is on the square and he was lying awake he heard a great concourse of people and following them a great discharge of arquebus fire that all seemed to him like more than 150 shots and from the voices and uproar this witness knew it must be the enemy and it could not be anything else since there was no armed guard in place in the city that night, and with all this he jumped up naked to grab his sword and dagger, and with them in hand he ordered one of his negroes to open the door, and having exited it, his house being across from the parish church he saw a great file of people alongside the said church that went all the way around the town council building and in the front of the said main church and they seemed to be in battle formation, which was confirmed when they fired arquebuses at him upon seeing him, but by the grace of God no bullet hit him, with which this witness returned to his house, seeing that he could not go out to join in the defense, as it seemed from the arquebus fire that the whole town was surrounded and under siege, and having closed his door and gotten dressed this witness heard a new sound at his door and near his house and having good quarter and seeing himself alone they offered him this [quarter] and he

offered himself as a prisoner after they gave him a few belt lashings that
left him with two wounds, one on the face and the other on his left arm,
and they told him: "You're not Juan Gonzáles, you're a rich man! Bring out
your silver!" And straightaway they sacked his house, robbing him of all
the wrought silver he had as well as the coined, which was little, and his
firearms and swords and daggers they broke apart so that they were use-
less, and having done this they grabbed this witness, his wife, and family
and the valuables and they took them to the house of Field Marshal Don
Pedro de Ocón, where they held him already a prisoner along with other
people, and they stayed there until 7 a.m. more or less. And with all their
people they took the prisoners they'd taken, men, women, and children
and all the booty to the beach where they waited, and being surrounded
there on the beach they stopped, and soon there arrived a launch already
given over to the enemy that appeared to belong to Damián de Orozco,
who arrived in it, with which surprise, this new embarkation, they, seeing
the prisoners and pillage, returned to attack the city, and there went back
to it more than 40 soldiers, who then remained on the beach with new
booty, including imported cloth and household furnishings, all of it carried by the Jaltebaños Indians, and those of Masaya and Nindirí whom
they found there, and among them the [Indian] magistrate Guillén who is
from Jalteba, and of this second sacking the said Indians took advantage,
and he has heard that some mulattoes did as well, more so since the enemy
cared little about the textiles, and the said Indians robbed the houses of
this city so thoroughly that they left nothing of value inside them, and this
witness suffered more from this robbery of textiles by the Indians than he
did by the English in silver, and to quite a degree. And being on the beach
around three in the afternoon they embarked some women, and they
wanted to embark them all in turns, taken by the Indian Gallardo, native
of the island of Solentiname, pilot as he has been of the said river and lake,
whom this witness knew must have come as guide [for the English]. This
one had been branded a slave in this city and made to work in the hospital
as a result of a murder he had committed, and to the call of other Englishmen who intended to take away the women, this same Englishman was
interrupted by the general call "Let's gather up all the ecclesiastical prisoners" and having made [the women] disembark they took on board this
witness, Field Marshal Don Pedro de Ocón, the prior of the San Juan de
Dios hospital, and magistrate of this city Captain Francisco de Mena, and
with these four, having loaded up all the pillage, which according to what
this witness could see and what others assumed it amounted to 150,000

pesos, a little more or less, and they retired to the little islands that lay about a league from the city, saying they carried the four of us for the security of their persons, fearing that we might bring some surprise upon them, and the next day around 7 a.m. they dispatched this witness, the field marshal, the padre prior, taking with them the said Captain Francisco de Mena, afterwards dropping them all off at their country estates that they have on the banks of the lake some 25 leagues from the city where they could see what little was there due to the robbery by the said Indians which was more notable than that taken by the English, although not so substantial as what they did in ruining the city, and the things there most necessary for its vestments and those now in place. And when this witness returned to the city he saw that they had sacked the main church which had possessed very rich silver service and considerable ornamentation; they broke the box in which was stored the Holy Sacrament and they stole the sacred vessels, throwing the Most Holy Form on the altar. And this witness holds for certain that this invasion was done by the English enemy mostly because the city and river by which they came up, which is the principal means of entry, had no fortification. And the city and province have long called for its fortification. It was this rather than because of the lack of sentinels that the enemy managed to take it, and it would be much better for this city to fortify the river than to garrison a thousand men and place sentinels along the river. And thus he responds.

DOCUMENT 29

Henry Morgan's Articles of Agreement (1669)[5]

Buccaneers had a reputation for lawlessness, incessant brawling, and heavy drinking, but, as suggested by the following document, their leaders were often hardheaded businessmen. These articles of association were presumably a standardized text used by many, if not all, raiding gangs based in Jamaica at that time. The agreement was designed to maintain discipline and ensure a fair division of the expected plunder with premiums for rank and bravery as well as compensation for being crippled in action. It is signed by the commanders of all thirteen vessels that assembled

5. Source: Archivo General de Indias, Indiferente General 1600.

for a large-scale raid and also gives the names of the quartermasters who represented the crews. This particular copy fell into the hands of the Spaniards when they seized an English vessel off Campeche in August 1670.

Articles of agreement had, made and concluded by and between:

Henry Morgan, esquire, admiral and chief commander of a squadron of ships belonging to His Majesty's island of Jamaica, with the respective captains of the ships and vessels belonging to the said squadron (to say) Captain John Anssell, Captain Jeffrey Pennant, Captain Benjamin Serjant, Captain John Morris, Captain Edward Dempster, Captain Richard Norman, Captain Robert Deleander, Captain Richard Dobson, Captain Miles Sharpe, Captain Adam Brewer, Captain Peter Porter and Captain Isaac Rush, of the one party

And two men out of the respective companies belonging to the above-said captains, the which represent the whole (to say) Samuell Stoate and John Long, Nicholas Daniell and Roger Harbourt, John Davis and Richard Arpoole, Guy Grubbin, Zachariah Lincourt, William Gammon and Jacob Martin, Lawrence Browne and George Hayes, Edward Goff and John Atkinson, Philipp Desiene and George Freeborne, Peter Harris and Andrew Bowyer, Edward Watkins and Dudly Scott, Abraham Corbin and Ipseiorawas, Joseph Lebell, John Mapoo, John Walker and John Wells, of the other party, as follows (viz.):

Imprimis. It's agreed and concluded upon by and between the above-said parties that whatsoever gold, silver, pearl, jewels, rings, precious stones, ambergris and brazer, or other merchandises which are, or shall be, within the term of this voyage taken on shore, shall be equally divided man for man as free plunder.

2nd. It's agreed and concluded that what ship or ships shall be taken at sea within the term of this voyage, the tenths and fifteens being deducted, the fourth part of that goods are in the hold of such ship or ships shall be for the respective ships of this fleet and their owners, and the other three fourths to be equally divided amongst such ship's company generally, and in case that any vessel or ship shall be taken when in company at sea with the fleet, that ship or vessel so taking of her, shall for fair encouragement have free entrance and plunder (that is to say) all chests, bedding,

JOHAN MORGAN,
gebooren in de Provincie van Walles, in Engelandt
Generaal van de Roovers op Iamaica.

Portrait of Henry Morgan from the Dutch edition of *The Buccaneers of America*, 1678. John Carter Brown Library at Brown University.

seamen's clothes and arms, and also one tenth part of all merchants' goods which are aboard in hold of the said vessel, the rest to be divided as aforesaid.

3d. It's further agreed and concluded upon that whatsoever captain of this fleet, during the term of this intended voyage, shall in any fight, or landing of men, lose his ship or vessel, provided it be not through neglect, shall receive full satisfaction according to appraisement, which appraisement shall be made by two men of such ship's company in the fleet, or his choice of any vessel taken, not exceeding the value of his own so appraised, and the said captain of such vessel still enjoying his former benefit.

4th. It's further agreed and concluded that what person or persons soever shall by means of drunkenness, or any other manner or way, neglect, slight or deny the reasonable commands of his or their officer or officers in either duty or duties, shall lose or forfeit his or their share or shares, or such punishment as shall by the Council of War be thought most convenient, as also on the other side what captain or captains governor that shall, by any manner of ways, neglect his or their duty or duties shall incur and forfeit the like personally.

5th. It's further agreed and concluded by and between the said parties that whatsoever shall loose a leg or an arm, or other limbs in the term of this voyage, so that it be made appear upon the oaths of two chirurgeons that that person or persons are disabled of getting of a future livelihood, share and receive out the whole 120 pounds sterling, or six able slaves to the value, or in other goods and merchandises if so much taken.

6th. It's agreed upon that whatsoever person or persons first espies a sail and makes the first sight so that it be made a prize, shall have for his encouragement twenty pounds sterling, or double share of plunder.

7th. It's agreed and concluded upon that whatsoever canoe or canoes be sent out from any ship or vessel in the fleet and take any purchase not exceeding the value of 200 pounds sterling, shall be divided among the canoe or canoes' crew for taking it, but if more then to be divided between the whole parties.

8th. It's concluded that what rigging, sails, cables, anchors or other necessaries belonging to a ship or vessel be taken shall be equally divided to every ship according to their proportion.

9th. It's further agreed and concluded that in case we should meet with any strong opposition in any place or places whatsoever that we are intended and bound for, as castles, fortresses or other stronghold, the first man entering such place shall have twenty pounds sterling, also he that first displayed his colors in such place as aforesaid twenty pounds sterling, for every grenade fired and break in such castles twenty shillings, as also to all those that carry ladders, for every ladder so carried and pitched up against the walls so that we can enter such castle, fortress or strong places, have ten pounds sterling.

10th. It's further agreed upon by and between the said parties that, out of the whole or general plunder, shall be deducted and taken out five men's shares and the same to be given to the Admiral for his care and expense over us.

11th. It's further agreed that that vessel or ship in any harbor or road shall be found to be aground or afloat, if laden, or whatsoever on board the said ship or vessel as aforesaid, the same shall be deemed as plunder taken off the shore, further if any ship or vessel aforesaid that shall be found in any harbor or road within the command of our enemy that canoe or canoes' crew or crews that shall fetch her off shall have one tenth part through all, if fetched off by any vessel or ship they to have one fifth part, as also any goods or merchandises, money, plate which shall in the time of our attempting of any pound or plate, or after we are descried, be put aboard if any ship or vessel or boat in any harbor or road by the enemy if taken, and then surprised by us, the same so taken shall be share as plunder taken off the shore.

12th. It's further agreed and concluded upon by and between the above-said parties that, for the true performance of all and every the above-written articles, we do bound ourselves, and every or either of us jointly or severally, our heirs, executors and administrators in the personal sum of 10,000 pounds sterling, money of England, to be received of him or them that shall anyways transgress or break the above-written articles, as witness our hands and seals the 8th day of January, in the year of our Lord [1669].

Henry Morgan, John Anssell, Geffry Pennant, Benjamin Sergant, John
Morris, Edward Dempster, Richard Norman, Robert Delander, Miles
Sharpe, Richard Dobson, Adam Brewer, Peter Porter, Isaac Rush.

DOCUMENT 30

A Buccaneer Describes Henry Morgan's Assault on Panama (1671)[6]

*In December 1670, five months after England and Spain had
agreed to the Peace of Madrid, which was meant to end all hostilities in the Caribbean, Henry Morgan assaulted Panama with a
large multinational gang consisting of more than 2,000 freebooters in thirty-eight vessels. About 1,400 men followed Morgan on
the long and arduous way across the isthmus. In the course of this
attack one of the most important cities in the Spanish empire was
burned to the ground. The spoils, however, were bitterly disappointing. Despite the fact that the raid must have been the talk
of the town in Port Royal, Jamaica, for weeks, if not months, only
two written accounts survive in the archives. The following narrative by an otherwise unknown man presents the incursion as a
paramilitary operation in wartime.*

Copy of the Relation of William Fogg concerning the action of the privateers in Panama taken on April 4, 1671

Says:

The 6 of December they sailed from Cape Tiburon and went directly
for the island of Providence, where they found 300 men in garrison, who
yielded next day upon quarter of life and liberty, only about 60 slaves
which the party had and about 500 pounds in plunder, where they stayed
one week, but in five days sent away Captain Bradley with 400 men to
take Chagre Castle, and seven days after they arrived in sight of the castle,
and after two days time they landed a league to windward of the castle,
and about three o'clock in the afternoon they came to the castle and gave

---

6. Source: The British Library, Add. Ms. 11410, fols. 159–60.

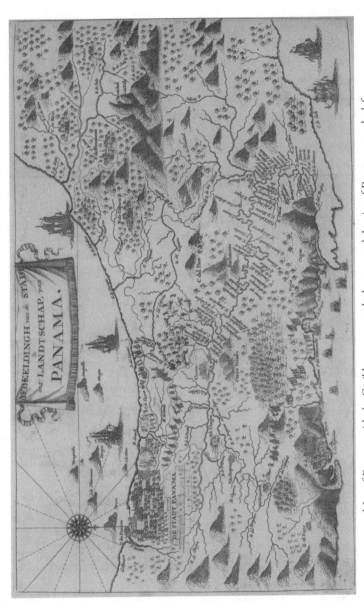

Map of Panama with the Caribbean coast at the bottom and the city of Panama near the left margin. Chagre Castle is located in the center of the bottom coastline. Tobago and Tobagillo are small islands off the Pacific coast, John Carter Brown Library at Brown University.

them a volley and fell into the trench, which was 12-foot deep, and that night they fired the castle, which made it so hot they could not enter, the same being of double palisades and thatch and ten-foot thick so they lay under the walls that night, and the next day—the third day—in the morning they fell on early in the morning and were beaten back, the enemy being 370 men, near as many as themselves, but our party rallied and returned upon them, entered the castle, and put all to the sword, saving none but slaves and such as hid themselves, none of the enemy's officers being saved. In this conflict we lost Captain Bradley, a brave man, Lieutenant Powell, and 150 men killed.

A week after the taking of this castle, the admiral having been retarded by contrary winds, came up to us, and at the entry over the bar the admiral and five small vessels and one sloop were cast away, and about ten men drowned, the sea running very high. Ten days after the admiral arrived, they prepared to go up the River Chagre in five vessels, which carried them about five leagues up the river, and after that they put their necessaries in canoes and some men, the rest marching the other five leagues by the river side, cutting the path with difficulty, finding five breastworks in the way, which the enemy left, and only gave them an ambuscade between the breastwork and the landing place, and fired on them and wounded two men and ran away, and so in five days they came to Venta de Cruces, which is the landing place where they found all burnt and lay there that night, and finding the next morning they were about 1,200 men, they marched (without having any intelligence of an enemy) and about three in the afternoon were ambuscaded by 1,000 Indians in a wood in the savanna on high ground, but our men ran up to the banks to them and put them to flight. In this we had one man killed outright and two hurt, and they lost their commander, the prince of the Indians, and about 30 men. A little from this place the party lay that night, and next day they marched about six miles and saw the enemy, both horse and foot, at a great distance, and the third they did the like, and toward the evening they saw the enemies in great numbers before and behind them, and found by their shouts they were within three miles of the enemy's camp.

The next morning our party marched up, being drawn up into three divisions, where they found the enemy ready to receive them, being about 2,000 foot and 700 horses. The horses were in two divisions that charged our forlorn and the right wing, both at once. But both parties of horse having received much loss by our first volley fled, and their foot gave one volley and fled after them, and we had the pursuit about three miles within a mile and a half of the town of Panama, in which the enemy lost 500 men and we one Frenchman.

That night our party entered the town and found the houses fired by the enemy and all in a flame, lodging that night in the churches and monasteries, which were of stone, and some houses that escaped the fire, and lay there a week searching victuals, etc., of which was plenty, but all the goods burnt and plate conveyed away, except some inconsiderable things. After this our men marched out in parties, sometimes 100, sometimes 40, and sometimes 10 in a party, and took prisoners every day, but never saw an enemy to face them.

After 28 days stay they marched the same way they came up, and so returned to Chagre. Whence a month since they sailed in company with the fleet, and three days after the said vessel came. Left the admiral about Portobelo, who had with him three sails. The rest went home to leeward, some to windward, and he supposes all that could make the best of their way for Jamaica.

The party got but ten pounds sterling per man in money and plate, besides negroes, etc.

DOCUMENT 31

Alexandre Exquemelin Describes the Same Raid (1678)[7]

Since the share that each robber in Panama received was bitterly disappointing, rumors emerged that Morgan had embezzled a large part of the spoils. Against this background, one participant in the looting, Alexandre Exquemelin, left the marauders and made his way back to Europe. He was a Frenchman who had come to Tortuga in 1666 as an indentured servant, but like so many others soon thereafter joined a raiding gang. He had probably participated in several raids and, in 1678, published a book about the buccaneers, which contains a bleak account of their actions and behavior in Panama. Certain details may be exagger-

7. Source: Alexandre-Olivier Exquemelin, *De Americaensche Zee-Roovers* (Amsterdam: Jan ten Hoorn, 1678), 133–36. (Translation Arne Bialuschewski, with thanks to Ernst Pijning.)

ated, but the core of the narrative, including the violence toward captives and the treatment of women, can be corroborated with scattered Spanish sources.

As soon as Morgan had seized complete control of Panama City, he sent out 25 men in a barque, which had previously been stranded at low tide in the harbor, as they have high and low water there, like in the English Channel. The harbor at high tide is so deep that a galleon can enter, but at low tide the sea is a mile away, leaving nothing but mud. At noon Morgan secretly ordered houses in various parts set afire, but started a rumor that the Spaniards themselves had done this. By nightfall most of the city was burning. Some tried to check the inferno by blowing up houses, but this was futile. The fire was so intense that, once the flames reached a street, within half an hour it was entirely engulfed, and soon after in embers. Most of the houses, including the finest, were made of wood, usually cedar, and contained priceless paintings that the Spaniards had been unable to send away. There were seven monasteries and a convent, together with a hospital and cathedral and a parish church, embellished with wonderfully rich paintings and sculpture, although the monks had taken all the silver work away with them. The city had about 2,000 houses belonging to affluent merchants as well as about 3,000 ordinary dwellings in addition to stables

The Sack of Panama, 1670–1671. John Carter Brown Library at Brown University.

for the pack animals, which carried silver cross-country to the north coast. In the suburbs were orchards and gardens full of fruit trees and vegetables. The Genoese maintained a large building there for their trade in negroes, but this was burnt along with the rest. By the next day the whole city was reduced to ashes, including about 200 warehouses and the stables for the pack animals, which stood some distance away. All the animals inside had been burnt and so had many slaves who hid in the houses and had not been able to escape. The great piles of flour sacks inside the warehouses were still smouldering a month afterwards.

That night the rovers camped around the city in case the Spaniards would come back, as they had been alarmed to find how greatly they were outnumbered. The next day all the wounded were brought to the monastery church, which was still intact and thereafter served as a guardhouse. All the guns were rounded up and mounted outside this church. Morgan drew up his men in battle order to assess what casualties had been sustained. About twenty men had been killed during the raid and as many wounded. Morgan sent a detachment of 150 men later that day to deliver the news of his victory to Chagre Castle. The main force escorted this detachment out of the city. Scattered groups of Spaniards observed them from a safe distance, but fled as soon as the rovers showed signs of closing in on them.

Toward noon Morgan and his men once more entered the city and took up quarters wherever they could. One band of men went around searching the charred ruins where they found a fair amount of silverware and silver coins, which the Spaniards had hidden in their cisterns. The following day two more parties, each of 150 men, left for the countryside to discover where the citizens had hidden themselves. Two days later they came back, bringing with them 200 captives, men and women, including slaves. The same day saw the return of the barque Morgan had sent out together with three seized vessels, but they had let their best prize slip through their fingers. It was a galleon loaded with the King of Spain's silver along with all the jewels and treasure of the foremost merchants in Panama. There were also nuns on board, carrying their church ornaments as well as their silver and gold. This ship was armed with only seven cannon and a dozen muskets. It was not even fully rigged as it lacked topsails and was moreover short of drinking water. The rovers learned of all these facts when they captured a boat that had been sent ashore from this galleon with seven men in it to fetch water. According to these men, the great ship could not possibly put to sea without water. The commander of the rovers, however, had been more inclined to sit drinking and carousing with a group of Spanish women he had taken prisoner rather than immediately pursue the treasure ship.

Next day he did have the barque made ready to hunt down the galleon, but without success. The ship had sailed away when the Spaniards aboard found out that the rovers were at sea and had captured the ship's boat. When they realized the galleon was out of reach, the men in the barque instead captured several boats laden with merchandise that they encountered near the islands of Tobago and Tobagilla before returning to Panama. On arrival they told Morgan what had happened. The prisoners from the ship's boat, when questioned, said they knew where the galleon was bound, but assumed that reinforcements would have arrived by now. At this news Morgan had all the vessels in Panama harbor fitted out to give chase. Once more the rovers put to sea, this time in four barques with 120 men aboard. They were at sea for eight days, but in vain, the great ship eluded them. Since there was no hope of catching up, they decided to return to Tobago and Tobagilla, and there they came across a ship from Paita laden with soap, cloth, biscuit and sugar, and carrying about 20,000 pieces of eight. They brought this prize back to Panama together with all the goods and prisoners they had taken in the islands.

The men Morgan had sent to Chagre Castle returned with good news. The garrison at Chagre had dispatched two vessels to cruise the coast near the river estuary where they had caught sight of a Spanish ship and had given chase. Since the rovers in the fortress had hoisted the Spanish flag, the fleeing ship, hard pressed, sought refuge in the river mouth. Hardly being able to escape one wolf, it ran into another's mouth: As soon as the river was reached, the Spaniards discovered they were under the guns of their enemy. Most of the captured cargo was food, which pleased the rovers as the garrison had been on short rations.

The news encouraged Morgan to stay longer in Panama and thoroughly loot the province. While some of his men went pillaging by sea, others scoured the countryside. A party of 200 men went out each day, and as soon as one expedition came back another was ready to depart. From these raids they brought back considerable booty and many prisoners, whom they tortured day by day in an effort to make them disclose where they had hidden their wealth. One of their captives was a frail man whom they found in a gentleman's house outside the city. This unfortunate man was wearing a good shirt he had found in the house along with a pair of silk breeches. A silver key was tied to the points of these breeches.

When the rovers asked him about the chest to which the key belonged, he told them he did not know and had simply found the key in the house. As soon as it became clear that he would not tell them more, they applied the strappado to him until both his arms were entirely dislocated, then knotted a cord so tightly around his forehead that his eyes bulged out as big as eggs. Since he still would not divulge the location of the chest, they hung him by his male parts, while one struck him, another sliced off his nose, yet another an ear, and another scorched him with fire. These tortures were as barbaric as any man could imagine. Finally, when the wretch could no longer speak and they could not think of new torments, they had a negro stab him to death with a lance. They committed many more similar atrocities. They showed little mercy, even to the monks, and would have shown none at all but for the hope of extracting money from them. They did not spare the women either, except for those who surrendered themselves willingly. The rovers had a way of dealing with any woman who held out. They would let her leave the church, which was being used as their prison, as if giving her a chance to go and wash herself, but once she was in their hands they would work their will upon her, or beat her, starve her, or similarly torment her. Morgan should have set a better example as their commander, but he was no better than the rest. Whenever a beautiful prisoner was brought in, he would dishonor her at once.

DOCUMENT 32

Henry Morgan Joins the War on Freelance Raiders (1677)[8]

After 1670 the colonial authorities in Jamaica slowly began to turn against the rogue privateers. Henry Morgan was sent as prisoner to London, but he was never tried and his political connections helped him in 1675 to return as lieutenant governor to Jamaica. The so-called sugar revolution, meanwhile, had created an enormous demand for slaves, and planting became a profitable business. Morgan continued to maintain close ties to the marauding community. Along with the colonial assembly,

---

8. Source: Longleat House, Coventry Papers 75, fols. 199–202.

however, he also reacted to mounting pressure from planters as well as the motherland and enacted the first law against raiding excesses. At the root of the problem was the fact that freebooters often obtained questionable privateering commissions from other countries, which made it virtually impossible to bring outlaws to justice. This issue was never more apparent than in April 1677 when James Browne, a Scotsman who operated under a French commission, seized a Dutch slave vessel and brought it along with its human cargo to Jamaica. Following this incident, Morgan outlined his policy in a letter to Sir Henry Coventry, then secretary of state and one of the most influential politicians in England.

St. Jago de la Vega, June 26, 1677

Most honored Sir,

In my last, I gave your honor an account of the Assembly being sitting, which have done little more than passing twelve acts that only concern this place and likewise this act which I herewith send your honor. We hope it will answer our expectations in recalling His Majesty's subjects from the service of foreign princes, which if it should not, there will be no way left but to repel them by force.

I hope likewise that this will so far satisfy the Spanish ambassador that he will have no occasion to think that they are any ways countenanced by anybody here, but that everyone will do their best to repel them. For my own part, if they should not come in the obedience of His Majesty, I think they deserve no favour. And if His Majesty in his prudence shall think fit to send two small frigates to repel them and be pleased to lay his commands upon me, I will follow them from place to place till I either bring them in or destroy them.

I gave your Honor an account by my last of a hundred and odd negroes that were punctually taken from the Dutch. They still remain in the custody of the provost marshall, and likewise those that took them. How His Excellency will proceed in it, I know not, but when it's over, I shall not fail to give your honor an account of it. I wish you increase of honor and felicity and assure you that my ambition is to demonstrate to you that I am with much zeal and sincerity,

Most honored sir,

Your most obliged, humble and faithful servant,

Henry Morgan

An Act declaring it felony without benefit of clergy for any person to serve under any foreign Prince or State

Whereas nothing can contribute more to His sacred Majesty's honor in all the treaties of peace than that such articles there concluded and agreed on should by all His Majesty's subjects, according to their duty, be most inviolably preserved and kept in and over all His Majesty's dominions and territories.

And whereas not only against such treaties made by His Majesty with his allies, but also contrary to His Sacred Majesty's royal proclamation, several of His subjects have and do continually go off this His Majesty's island into foreign princes' services and sail under their commissions, it being contrary to their duty and good allegiance.

And whereas by fair means they cannot be restrained from so doing.

Be it enacted by the Governor, Council and Representatives of the Commons of this island assembled, and it is hereby enacted by the authority of the same:

That, from and after the publication hereof, it shall be felony for any person which now does or hereafter shall inhabit or belong to this island to serve in an hostile manner under any foreign prince, state or potentate, or any employed under any of them, without special license for so doing under the hand and seal of the Governor or Commander in Chief of this island for the time being.

And that all and every such offender and offenders, contrary to the true intent of this act, being thereof duly convicted in His Majesty's Supreme Court of Judicature within this island, shall suffer pains of death as a felon without benefit of clergy.

Provided nevertheless that this act or anything herein contained shall not extend to any person or persons now in the service or employment of any foreign prince or state whatever that shall come to this island and leave or desert such service or employment within twelve months after the publication hereof, but that all such shall be fully indemnified for anything they have acted or done, and shall be free in their persons and estates from any debts they now owe within this island, until the full end and time of five years from their so coming in as aforesaid be expired.

And that nothing in this act be construed to extend to any inhabitant of this island who shall help wood, water, pilot or assist any allies of His

Majesty in such like necessity anything herein contained to the contrary
in anywise notwithstanding.

DOCUMENT 33

A French Participant Describes the
Raid on Veracruz (1683)[9]

*In early 1683 a multinational raiding force ventured to loot the
vessel that sailed every year to Honduras, but the operation was
spoiled when one crew assaulted the target before all cargo
was on board. The freebooters next decided to launch a large-
scale attack on Veracruz, Mexico's most important Caribbean
port. They circumvented the main fortification and apprehended
about 1,500 inhabitants, mostly black people. An attempt to
ransom all captives, however, was aborted when a Spanish fleet
approached. The attackers withdrew hastily and could not replenish their supplies. The following account was attached to a letter
dated November 13, 1683 from Pierre Arnoul, the intendant of
the Marine in Rochefort in the southwest of France. An unnamed
Frenchman describes the turbulent events before, during, and
after the raid when the marauders struggled to find suitable markets where they could dispense of their spoils.*

Relation of a freebooter voyage to Honduras and New Spain

Captains Laurens de Graaf and Michel Andreson, commanding two vessels of 30 guns and 150 men each, with a longboat, set sail in the month
of November 1682 and called at the island Roatán, where they careened
their vessels while waiting for the Honduras hulk coming out of the
River Amatique. There they were joined by about 100 men in canoes led
by Jean Blot and Jan Willems. At the beginning of April, Nicolaes van
Hoorn, commanding a ship of 40 pieces of cannon and 300 men, seized
the hulk along with the accompanying patache in the river mouth. The

---

9.   Source: Archives nationales, Marine B⁴ 9, fols. 389–90. (Translation Arne
Bialuschewski.)

spoils consisted of 2,000 pounds of indigo. And after having plundered the hulk they removed the artillery and everything that seemed useful, said Van Hoorn set her on fire and equipped the patache with 24 cannon, which command he gave to Jean Tristan.

Then they all plotted together, with two or three English vessels that were there too, to go and surprise Veracruz, where they arrived on May 19 one hour before daybreak. They went ashore half a mile from that city, which they entered without encountering any resistance. There was only some fighting in the fortifications, which were seized swiftly. They demanded to surrender the fort San Juan de Ulúa, which controls the city, of which they were masters for five to six days, and would have remained longer, but they espied a fleet from Spain waiting for them. This forced them to withdraw earlier than planned to the small island of Sacrificio where they shared their loot consisting of 500,000 pieces of eight and 7,500 pounds of broken silver coins, around 36 cases of cochineal, and 1,200 negroes or mulattoes. When all vessels were at said island, said Van Hoorn and de Graaf had a dispute, and it came to a skirmish, the first was wounded in the arm, which he died of five or six days later, having left the command of his ship to Jean de Grammont, who had joined them from Petit-Goâve. Part of the English withdrew to Jamaica, while others sailed to Carolina. De Graaf, Andreson, Willems, and Blot, with a small prize seized by de Graaf in Honduras that was of little use, went to Petit-Goâve in late August, after much suffering from a lack of provisions and they lost many of their slaves, but said Sieur Grammont and Tristan were still at sea. Those who arrived believed that they had been forced to go to Carolina for provisions, even careen their ships there. Said de Graaf, Andreson, Willems, Blot and François Le Sage, commanding the small prize, were ready to get out of Petit-Goâve to go to Santiago de Cuba, which is the lair of the [Spanish] pirogues, which have much harassed us for five to six months. One of these privateers, with a crew of about 70 men, appeared about September 16 or 18 at Cape Tiburon, and attacked an English vessel, which had 15 or 16 French freebooters on board, who had just lost de Graaf's longboat on the coast of Cuba, and these men fought back the Spaniards and would have even taken their pirogue if the wind had blown.

On the way from Petit-Goâve to Port-de-Paix we encountered three sloops full of hunters and inhabitants of the Cape, who left to join the freebooters, and others from Port-de-Paix had done the same for that purpose.

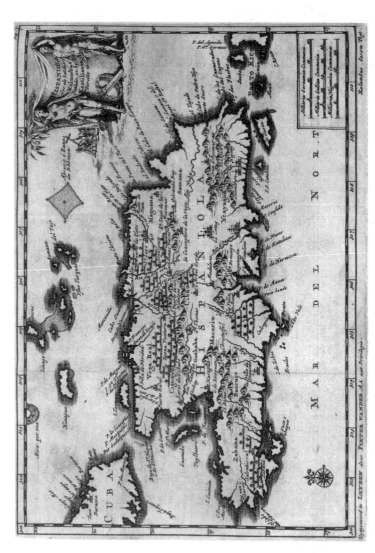

Map of Hispaniola showing Petit-Goâve on the north coast of the southwestern peninsula. Port-de-Paix is on the north coast opposite of Tortuga. John Carter Brown Library at Brown University.

DOCUMENT 34

Spanish Subjects Describe the Raid on Veracruz (1683)[10]

The sack of Veracruz aroused much attention all over the Caribbean and beyond, but communication was slow and often unreliable. It depended on sailing vessels carrying information from port to port, and eventually across the Atlantic. In this case incoherent, and in part contradictory reports, were gathered by the governor of Havana, from where the fleets left for Spain. His summary of the available information provides further details of the proceedings of the raiders that were not reported in France one month earlier. However, the fact that the raiders suffered from a lack of provisions and that many of their captives starved to death appears to have escaped the governor's attention.

Summary of writs, letters, and other papers that were remitted to the Council [of the Indies] by Don Joseph Fernández de Córdoba, the governor of the city of Havana, concerning the sack of the city of Veracruz by pirates in the preceding month of May of this year.

In a letter that the president of Santo Domingo wrote to the governor of Havana on March 30 of last year, he told him how an English captain had been in that port with his ship, and had sailed out to sea saying that he would burn down the city of Santiago de Cuba, and carry out other hostilities in [Cuba] in order to get satisfaction for the proceedings against him in that island for some excesses that it was confirmed he had committed, news which he was letting him know about for what it might be worth to the service of His Majesty, though he considered them idle and of little substance, though he did not specify the motive for the said proceedings.

And according to what is recognized by context of those writs, it seems that this same captain went to the province of Honduras to capture the great ship that was taking registered cargo to it from Spain, and although he didn't achieve it since the crew set it on fire and burned it, he took

---

10. Source: Archivo General de Indias, Santo Domingo 3, ramo 2, no. 66b. (Translation Marc Eagle.)

another smaller one that had gone in its company, armed it and brought it with him, and having joined with another pirate named Lorenzo, who it is said is French, and is the one who captured the frigate of the Armada de Barlovento named *La Francesa*, which he travels in, together they made various robberies and piracies on those coasts and on those of Campeche, and finally having sent to Petit-Goâve for 300 men in one of his ships, and having gathered some eleven or twelve vessels, four or five of them large and the rest medium-sized and small, and more than 1,000 men, they decided at the beginning of this May to go and sack the city of Veracruz, and did so, as will be told.

This news of the intent of these pirates came to the attention of the governor of Havana Don Joseph Fernández de Córdoba on the 30th of the same month of May, on the occasion of the arrival at that port of a corsair galliot whose commander was Antonio Martín, that on leaving Campeche encountered three small vessels of Englishmen that had come to cut wood in the place called las Cocinas, and after taking ten or twelve men prisoner in them they gave him that news, and since he didn't have the means to sustain them and some were sick and others injured, he left them on shore and took those three vessels with him to Havana, where the governor took a declaration from him and others about what has already been described that they had heard from those who were on the captured ships.

And the next day, May 31, with testimony of all the abovementioned writs, the governor of Havana dispatched a vessel to Veracruz with letters for the viceroy the Marqués de la Laguna, the governor of that city, the castellan of San Juan de Ulúa, and the treasury officials, giving all of them warning of the pirates' intent so that they might be prepared.

But these measures did not succeed, since by this time the said pirates had already sacked [Veracruz], which according to what was related by two slaves and an Indian who were present, in the following manner.

On the 17th of May they say that the two pirates arrived at the coast of Veracruz with twelve large and small ships and up to 1,000 men, most of them French, and disembarked up to 800 or 900 of them at the place called Punta Gorda about 7 at night, and having arrived at the city and surrounded it in their first advance, they fired all their musketry, killing over 100 people, and overpowered the city and made fortifications in its plaza for the space of five days, in which time they took everything they found in it of gold, silver, indigo, cochineal, and other things, and with [this booty] and the prisoners they took, which would be around 1,500 people of all sexes and ages, they went on board their vessels and held them at Isla de Sacrificios, and there they divided up the silver from the sack and distributed the prisoners among all twelve of their ships, and after eight days they spotted twelve or thirteen sails one afternoon, and fearing that it might be the naval fleet (as it actually was) they fled back toward Tabasco, sending the large ships away and the medium and small vessels along the coast, in order to meet up in the place called Manzanilla and split up there the cochineal and the slaves they had taken prisoner, and they were saying that afterwards they would have to gather up people again in Petit-Goâve and go back to see if they could take the city of Havana—these three witnesses don't describe what the sack was worth or who was killed, and don't give any specific details other than what has been related.

And it seems that one of the twelve vessels of the pirates, which was a barque with two sails carrying 22 Frenchmen and 44 or 48 prisoners, most of whom were women, after arriving near the city of Trinidad on the coast of Cuba on August 2 of this year hit a reef and ruptured, and the 22 Frenchmen and one woman saved themselves in the ship's boat, and two blacks, three Indians and one mulatto saved themselves using the ship's spars and made it to land, and with this news the lieutenant governor of that city sent out four canoes, two of them armed in order to follow the boat of the Frenchmen, and the other two to go to the place where the ship ran aground and collect any other people that might have survived, and four women and four boys were found alive and taken to the city, and all the others had been drowned, and it is not said whether they met up with the boat of the Frenchmen.

And of those who were saved from this ship, the said lieutenant governor examined the two black slaves that it was previously said were in Veracruz at the time while the sack was carried out, and the Indian, a native of the city of Granada in Nicaragua, who had been traveling as a prisoner with those pirates for over two years previously, and from their declarations what has already been said is on record, and the lieutenant sent them to the governor of Havana with a letter of the 4th of August referring to the news obtained from them.

On the 9th and 13th of August the governor of Havana examined another two witnesses, and the commander of the port of Matanzas wrote two letters, both of which concern giving news of the sack of Veracruz, and since what they contain is hearsay of people who couldn't be examined since they weren't there, and everything can be reduced to what has already been said as declared by the two slaves and the Indian, more specific mention of its contents is not made, if indeed the particular details they add are that the enemy entered Veracruz undetected, and that the sack was worth a million and a half, outside of the prisoners, who were more than 1,300 not including the dead, that they took the silver from the royal treasury, and that after robbing whatever they found, they made the priest of Veracruz go up in the pulpit and exhort the citizens to surrender everything to the pirates that they had hidden, since if they didn't they would put them all to the sword, and with this fear they surrendered great amounts, and that they treated the governor very badly, cutting off his hair and beard out of spite, and that they made one rich resident carry his own valuables in order to put it aboard the ships, in which they made him work so much that he died from exhaustion, and that after all this they carried off the governor and treasury officials, for whose ransom they asked 150,000 pesos, which had to be given within eight days, and that they were actually paid on the seventh, and that the said pirate went with his men and prisoners to the island of Roatán where he had settled and had much farmland, or wanted to settle to have a land of his own, and the other Dutch pirate went to an island next to Trinidad to the windward, although one witness says that he heard that there had been some arguments between the two main pirates, over which they had a falling out, and went on shore at the Laguna de Términos, and that Lorenzo had killed the Dutchman.

All these circumstances as said above are related as hearsay, and not everyone responds in them, since some of them say some things, and others others, and it is hearsay of hearsay and not of persons who were there during the sack.

And the governor of Havana, in a letter that he writes to His Majesty dated the 14th of that month of August, gives account of all that has been related, with the writs that were mentioned, and the president of the Casa de la Contratación [Royal Trade Office] Don Juan Ximénez de Montalvo and the tribunal of the Casa itself also write in letters of the 30th of this previous November informing about the news they received about that sack, but there are no other writs than the ones that the said governor of Havana remits, which were described, signed in Madrid on December 13, 1683

Licenciate Don Juan de Vallejo y Barcena

DOCUMENT 35

A Buccaneer Offer of Friendship after Veracruz (1683)[11]

After the successful raid of Veracruz, the attackers quickly dispersed. The Dutchman Laurens de Graaf, who was about to become the most successful freebooter of his day, first called at Point Negril in the west of Jamaica and then sailed on to Petit-Goâve in the south of Saint-Domingue, where sugar plantations grew all over the land. He understood that freelance raiders depended on access to colonial ports where they needed to exchange plunder for supplies. Furthermore, in the international conflicts of the late seventeenth century alliances between European powers shifted frequently, and today's enemy could be tomorrow's friend. Thus de Graaf did his best to keep his options as open as possible for future ventures.

Sir Thomas Lynch, Royal Governor of Jamaica

Sir,

I am much obliged for your civility and thank you for the honor which you have been pleased to do me without any merit of my own. I beg you to believe me the most humble of your servants, and to employ me if there be any place or occasion in which I can be of service to you. You will see how I shall try to employ myself.

Sir, I implore you very humbly, if by chance, I should go to your coast in quest of necessities for myself or my ship. I beg that my interests may be protected and no wrong done me, as I might do so if the opportunity presented itself for doing you service. Hoping for this favor, I remain forever,

Sir,

Your most humble and affectionate servant,

De Graffe

At Petit-Goâve, this 3rd September 1683

---

11. Source: The National Archives, Colonial Office 1/52, fol. 215. (Translation Arne Bialuschewski.)

Map of Jamaica with Port Royal, formerly Point Cagway, on the long peninsula at the eastern bay on the south coast and Point Negril at the western tip of the island. John Carter Brown Library at Brown University.

QUESTIONS TO CONSIDER FOR SECTION V:

What conditions gave rise to a raiding culture in the Caribbean?

How did the buccaneers portray themselves?

What image do we gain of Henry Morgan from various sources?

Were buccaneers engaged in warfare or simply plunder?

SECTION VI: THE SOUTH SEA RAIDERS

In April 1680, when raiding in the Caribbean waned, a group of three hundred men led by Richard Sawkins and Bartholomew Sharpe crossed the Isthmus of Panama and seized Spanish vessels, which enabled them to pillage targets all along the Pacific coasts of Central and South America. Even though the spoils were limited, in the following decade more English and Frenchmen went to the so-called South Sea or Pacific Ocean to assault the Spaniards who were hardly prepared to defend coastal shipping and port towns against hostile intruders. Thus the number of vessels that the raiders seized was considerable, but the plunder was mostly disappointing. When the pirates became increasingly frustrated by their lack of success, some sought new targets elsewhere. On their voyages the men advanced into parts of the Spanish empire that were barely known to the outside world. After their return to England and France a few marauders presented themselves as adventurers and published accounts of their raiding voyages.

DOCUMENT 36

Pirates Capture the *Rosario* (1681)[1]

When the freebooters sailed up and down the South Sea coast of the Americas, they seized one Spanish vessel after the other, yet the spoils remained disappointing. This was in part due to the fact that colonial authorities focused on the defense of treasure vessels, but bad luck and incompetence also played a role. Above all, the raiders acquired valuable geographical information that helped subsequent intruders penetrate the region and seize richer prizes. The following document, published in an amended and updated English version of Exquemelin's book, was probably

---

1. Source: *Bucaniers of America: or, A True Account of the Most Remarkable Assaults Committed of Late Years upon the Coasts of the West-Indies* (London: William Crooke, 1684), book III, 79–81.

written by William Dyck after he had been imprisoned in London and acquitted in a questionable piracy trial in June 1682. Based on journals that the marauders brought with them, the author chronicled the raiding voyage along the western seaboard of Central and South America.

In June 1681 we cleaned our vessel in the gulf called Dulce, which we had not done so long before, and you may easily believe was by this time very foul. Having sailed from thence toward Cape of San Francisco, somewhere about that cape, in July we took a ship that was bound for Panama, and was laden with cacao nuts, and had besides, some small quantity of plate on board her. We took out of her the plate and goods, and what else we pleased, cut down the main mast, and so let her go before the wind toward the port she was bound unto. About a fortnight after, at Cape Pasado, we took another small prize which was bound for Paita or Lima, that being the harbor, or landing place of all that goes up to that great city, the head of Peru. This was only a kind of packet boat that was going from Panama to Paita. She ran in under the shore when we gave her chase, and most of the passengers and other people got to land, but we took the greatest part of them, and dismissed them the next day, not knowing what to do with them, so they were forced to foot it over land back again to Panama. The vessel likewise we turned loose before the wind, the next day after we had rummaged her pretty well, as having no further service for her.

The next after we came up with another sail at Cape Pasado (where we took the packet boat), which proved to be one of the greatest adventures of this whole voyage, if not the greatest at all, had we but known our happy fortune, and how to make good use of it. This was a ship called *Santo Rosario*, or the *Holy Rosario*, of an indifferent big burden, and loaded with brandy and oil, wine and fruit, besides good store of other provisions. They fired at us first, but we came up board to board with them, and gave them such volleys of small shot, that they were soon forced to surrender, having several of their men wounded, their captain killed, and one only man more. In this ship, besides the lading above-mentioned we found also almost 700 pigs of plate, but we took them to be some other metal, especially tin: and under this mistake they were slighted by us all, especially the captain, and seamen, who by no persuasions used by some few, who were for having them rummaged, could not be induced to take them into our ship, as we did most of other things. Thus we left them on board the *Rosario*, and not knowing what to do with the bottom, in that scarcity of men we were under, we turned her away loose unto the sea, being very glad we had got such good belly timber out of her, and thinking little what quantity of rich metal we left behind. It should seem this plate was not yet thoroughly refined and fitted for to coin, and this was the occasion that deceived us all. One only pig of plate, out of the whole number of almost 700, we took into our ship, thinking to make bullets of it; and to this effect, or what else, our seamen were pleased, the greatest part of it was melted or squandered away. Afterwards, when we arrived at Antigua, we gave the remaining part of it, which was yet about one third therof, unto a Bristol man, who knew presently what it was (though he dissembled with us), brought it for England, and sold it there for 75 pounds sterling, as he confessed himself afterwards to some of our men. Thus we parted with the richest booty we had gotten in the whole voyage, through our own ignorance and laziness.

In this ship, the *Rosario*, we took also a great book full of sea-charts and maps, containing a very accurate and exact description of all the ports, soundings, creeks, rivers, capes, and coasts belonging to the South Sea, and all the navigations usually performed by the Spaniards in that ocean. This book, it seemed, served them for an entire and complete Waggoner, in those parts, and for its novelty and curiosity was presented unto His Majesty after our return into England. It has been since translated into English, as I hear, by His Majestie's order, and the copy of the translation, made by a Jew, I have seen at Wapping, but withal the printing thereof is severely prohibited, lest other nations should get into those seas and make use thereof, which is wished may be reserved only for England against its due time. The seaman who at first laid hold of it on board the *Rosario* told us the Spaniards were going to cast this book overboard, but that he prevented them, which notwithstanding we scarce did give entire credit unto, as knowing in what confusion they all were. Had the captain himself been alive at that time, this his story would have deserved more belief; yet, howsoever, if the Spaniards did not attempt to throw this book into the sea, at least they ought to have done it for the reasons that are obvious to every man's understanding, and are hinted at before. We parted with the *Rosario* and her plate the last day of July 1681.

DOCUMENT 37

Richard Arnold Tells His Tale (1686)[2]

In 1684 and 1685 a second surge of English and French raiders crossed the Isthmus of Panama and entered the South Sea. There various gangs joined together and separated several times, sometimes along national lines. Some crossed the Pacific to seek opportunities in the Indian Ocean while others returned to Jamaica. Ultimately it appears that few South Sea raiders were apprehended by the authorities. Among the colonial correspondence there is a transcript of the remarkable narrative of one young man who provides us with a unique insight into the proceedings of various marauding gangs. This document shows how these bands were driven by insatiable greed for gold and silver, but acquiring provisions and other supplies was often the more immediate concern. The treatment of natives and people of African descent was opportunistic and depended on the circumstances. Conflicts broke out in times of scarcity and whenever the success of the entire venture seemed in doubt.

The examination of Richard Arnold
aged 26 years or thereabouts

This examinant says that on or about the 16th day of June Anno Domini 1684 he went off this island on a voyage for the South Sea under the command of one Captain Peter Harris, being invited to that undertaking by one John Matthews, an acquaintance of the said examinant, being the only man of all the company that went over with the said examinant who had been there before, and that the said Arnold went off in a sloop whereof one Daniel Smith was master from Point Negril to Grand Cayman and from thence to the Mosquitoes in another sloop where he was taken in by the said Harris on board his barque, and from thence transported to the main, near Golden Island, where they landed and mustered under the said Harris to the number of 96 white men and three Indians, and there sunk their vessels. On their arrival there they were told by the

---

2. Source: The National Archives, Colonial Office 1/60, fols. 34–37. (A different version survives in the Huntington Library, Blathwayt Papers BL 327.)

Indians that King Golden Cap was dead, which troubled them for some time, but were soon revived by the good news that one Josepho, a great man amongst them, spoke Spanish and had considerable command and interest among the Indians and was willing to be their guide through the country toward the stockades, whither they were designed, being about 30 leagues distance from their landing place, whereupon they set forward under the said Josepho's conduct having with him about 20 Indians and sent others before to prepare canoes for them, about 12 leagues above from the said stockades, and performed their march in fewer days and there embarked into the canoes provided as aforesaid, and so came down the river and landed within half a mile of the said stockades having along the way, by the help of the said Josepho, got together about 300 Indians, and early in the morning fell on the said place, and took it where they shared about 100 shares at 24 ounces of gold dust for a share leaving the other gross plunder to the Indians. At this place also they took a barque belonging to his most Catholic Majesty of four [cannon] and 30 men, well armed with small arms, with about 1,000 pounds sterling in gold dust, the rest of her cargo being liquors and lumber. Here also the said examinant says they took eight large canoes on which they also embarked again, leaving the Indians at the stockades, and so with their barque and canoes went down the River Andriel to the mouth of it, where they took another vessel laden with provisions and some wine with which they proceeded on their voyage for the cays to the southward of Panama, about two leagues thence called the King's Cays, where they took about ten sail of pearl barques, having nothing on board them but maize, plantains, etc. and with two of the best of the said barques and the other barque of four [cannon], being well fitted (out of the other eight) with all manner of necessary rigging, they proceeded to Cape Clare to the southward of Panama to cruise for a ship, leaving the other eight barques dry on the shore at the cays, from whence, having spent some time to no purpose, they steered away again to the westward, near the place from whence they fitted, where they were attacked by five barques fitted out from Panama, to take them but could not lash him fast, by reason they so well defended themselves with pikes, and the night coming on, whilst the rest of his fleet lay to windward and saw fair, in this engagement they lost three men outright, and two more wounded who died soon after, the Spanish admiral and about 40 men, from whence they stood away further to the westward for Nicoya in hopes of getting a bigger vessel, being a place where the Spaniards built their ships, in sight of which place they espied a ship at an anchor to which they made, and sent their canoe on board to know who or what she was, which proved to be Captain Swan in a ship of about 140 tons, 16 guns and 20 men, with whom they entered into an agreement, for his ship at ten shares himself at two, and his boy half a share (the business of the said Swan before that time, as this examinant believes, being only for trade) on which agreement they manned the said ship, and turned the lesser barques adrift, retaining only that first taken, and so stood away to the southward to join themselves with one Captain John Cooke, who the said Swan told them was come about in a Dutch ship of 36 guns (which he took with a small vessel of three guns on the coast of Guinea) and at the Isle of Plate found the said ship commanded by one Captain Davis,

Map of Darien in eastern Panama where Richard Arnold twice crossed the isthmus. Golden Island is near the right margin, and the River Andriel flows from the mountains to the South Sea. John Carter Brown Library at Brown University.

and manned with 75 men (the said Cooke being dead) on board of which ship the said Captain Davis had a prisoner, who undertook to carry them to a rich town called Guayaquil, on which voyage they proceeded, and went up the river in their canoes, and landed about 130, about two leagues short of the town where being landed, and ready to march on seeing many lights in the town, a dispute arose between the said Swan and Davis (who then commanded the whole party) Swan supposing the same to be lighted matches, would not adventure to march farther concluding they were descried whereupon they returned on board again, much dissatisfied with Swan's conduct, being well assured by their prisoners they might have made 500 pounds sterling a man in gold.

From this place they proceeded to another place, called Paita, where they also landed about 90 men, and took it, plundered and burned it, where also they were entertained with about 160 men from Piura, a place they designed to take by surprise so finding themselves descried, and that city in arms for their coming, they returned on ship board again. On this bad success it was generally concluded amongst them to stand away to the westward again for the cays of Lima, where they continued about five months.

During which time several parties came over land (as this examinant and his companies had done before them) and got to the said cays in canoes, viz. one Captain François [Grogniet] with about 400 French, Captain Lescuyer with about 50, both which came together over land from Golden Island as aforesaid, and to welcome the said [Grogniet], this examinant says they gave him a great ship of 400 tons, which they had taken whilst at the cays, laden with flour, where also they took about twelve barques with provisions, fowls, and other such like necessaries, bound for Panama, all which barques they turned adrift, having first taken their necessaries. After the arrival of the two former parties and disposal of the said great ship there came three other parties over land by way of Golden Island, viz. Captain Francis Townly, Captain Leigh, and Captain Branly with about 360 men amongst them, most English, who in his voyage with his canoes took two ships with provisions when it was further concluded to carry on the design against the Spanish fleet, and that Davis should be admiral (having an antiquated French commission) and carry the flag at main top mast head, and that Swan should be vice-admiral, who utterly refused to wear French colors or fight under any other colors than the King of England's for that he had lost three men in fair trade with the Spaniards and so wore the Union Flag at fore top mast head, King's Jack etc. and that Captain [Grogniet] should second Davis who was to lay the admiral on board Captain Townly to second Captain Swan who was to board the vice-admiral, and that Captain Leonard in a fire barque should also attend on Davis, if needed were to burn the Spanish admiral and in that manner to engage the Spanish fleet.

In the interim of which the Spanish fleet standing far off, in the offing, passed unseen and landed their men at La Villa, about ten leagues to the westward of Panama and there took considerable reinforcement of men etc. and came to sea consisting of about eleven sail and two fire ships, the admiral having 54 guns, vice-admiral 46, rear-admiral 36, and from thence to 26 and 16 guns coming unexpected to the privateers, about the cays from the westward stood right in upon them, which caused them to weigh and stand off to clear and get the wind of them, if possible, upon which the Frenchman who should have seconded Davis, bore away and never offered to tack or come to their assistance, whereby that day was quite spent without any action. The next day they being to leeward of the Spanish fleet, the admiral and his fleet bore down on Davis, who bore away to speak with Swan and Townly, and consult then what was fit to be done, who finding the French had left them and that the Spaniards were to windward of them with their fire ships, made a running fight of it, having turned some of their canoes adrift, and lost others, some by the Spaniards' shot, went further to the westward to a place called Quibdó, to build new canoes, where in three weeks time they built ten new ones, where it was concluded to go for Realejo, and the city of León, but Swan suspecting them not to be strong enough for both at once, they only fell on the city of León, which they took, plundered, and burned, having missed of the wealth, by being descried there they entered the town so shared no considerable matters.

After which they reassumed their former resolutions for Realejo, which they likewise took, plundered, and burned, the last place affording nothing valuable to them more than pitch or tar, and other naval stores, pitch and tar being the produce of those places and that place famous for building great ships. There also the Spaniards set fire to two considerable ships on the stocks, one ready to launch, to prevent their falling into the enemy's hands.

At this place the fleet divided, being in or about the month of June Anno Domini 1685. Swan and Townly directing their course farther to the westward, for Acapulco and California, to try their fortunes there, and from thence round by the Philippine Isles for the East Indies and for home (as they said). Captain Davis and his fire ship designing back again to the southward, for Trujillo, a place far to windward, after which this examinant never saw or heard of Swan and Townly in their designed voyage for Trujillo. Being in some want of provisions, Davis, with whom the examinant sailed, touched at certain islands called the Galapagos, being informed by some of the crew that Captain Eaton had formerly left some flour there, and accordingly found it true, and took in 700 packs of flour, and so proceeded for Trujillo, but missed of it, the winds blowing so hard tacking that it was not possible for them to turn to windward of it, or row ahead with their canoes, and so bore up for Zaña, about twelve leagues to leeward of them, and landed at a small port called Chérrepe and took it, with all the Indians belonging to that town to prevent being descried, and so marched for Zaña, being about seven leagues up in the country, with 230 men, commanded by Captain Davis and one Captain Knight, in a barque of 55 men (who fell in with them as they came from the westward) which town they took and kept it three days, and plundered it, where they shared about 300 pieces of eight a man in money and plate. In their return they found in a storehouse about 400 jars of wine and 10,000 weight of indigo, but meddled not with anything but a little liquor, the seas running too high to carry off any heavy matter. After which they concluded to fall on another inland town called Piura, about ten leagues to leeward of Zaña, and about the same distance in the country, and to that purpose being informed by their pilot of the scarcity of water by the way, had fitted themselves with calabashes to carry every man's portion of water, fit for the march, but were discovered by an Irishman, who was taken by the Spaniards as he was returning from Zaña to the ships, who confessed the design to the Spaniards, and never acquainted them with it, being let go again, but suffered them to proceed on it, and were going ashore in their canoes for Piura, when by chance they took a small barque, the master of which told them they were betrayed, and that the town was in arms for them, so they altered their purpose and fell on a town called Paita, which they formerly burned (where the said master told them were two ships, one with 500 negroes, the other with magazine goods and friars) and took the town and ships, but took not away above 39 negroes, and some goods for clothing, where the examinant also with 38 more of their company deserted the said Davis, resolving back again, on which the said Davis gave them two small barques to carry them back into the River Andriel. At the mouth of which river they left their barques, and bought six canoes from the Indians, and embarked on them having each of them a negro to carry their luggage over land, and after six days spent, in coming up the river, they arrived at the foot of the mountain above the stockades, and from thence in two days marched to a place called Matanzas, being about eight leagues from the said mountains, where they all divided again into small parties.

This examinant with five other English, viz. John Michel, William Ruyter, Samuel Leigh, William Neville, and Robert Dawes, betaking themselves to a canoe, being disturbed by a Spanish pirogue sent thither on purpose to interrupt their passage, and so designed in their canoe for the Mosquitoes, but off of Point Blanco, about 50 leagues to windward of the Mosquitoes, they met with a sloop, one Peter Courtney master, with whom they agreed to be put on ashore at Salt Tortudos, but the wind over blowing and not able to beat it up to windward, stood over for Jamaica, where they landed at Manatee Bay to leeward of Port Royal, and this examinant further says that he never saw Captain Eaton, but was told that he went about by the East Indies about six months before Swan left them. Neither did he hear anything more of the French that deserted them that he left about 250 men under the command of Captain Davis, amongst whom was Peter Harris with whom this examinant went over (who was related unto Peter Harris that was formerly killed in those parts) the said Captain Davis at the coming away of this deponent, designed to make an attempt upon [left blank: Cañete?] about seven leagues to the southward of Lima. After which it was resolved that he would fit his own ship in order to return (with such as would go with him) through the Straits of Magellan, when the rest have determined to return overland by way of Darien, for that it is the examinant's opinion that they will be all come away in less than fewer months from this time, and the examinant further says that they never settled in any island, or fortified the same, as had been reported, and that he arrived here on Saturday night, being the 24th July 1686 and further says not

Richard Arnold

Sworn before me this 4th August 1686
Hender Molesworth

QUESTIONS TO CONSIDER FOR SECTION VI:

What drove buccaneers to raid Spanish targets in the Pacific Ocean around 1680?

What patterns did they follow and what special challenges did they face?

How did the Spanish respond to buccaneer incursions in the Pacific?

SECTION VII: PIRATES IN THE INDIAN OCEAN

In the 1690s many raiders sought new targets in the Indian Ocean. The most spectacular success occurred in August 1695 when Henry Avery pillaged two vessels belonging to a rich Muslim pilgrim fleet. He later vanished with substantial spoils and became an example that an entire generation of pirates endeavored to emulate. In the following years about 1,500 marauders from the American colonies sailed to the Indian Ocean, and Madagascar emerged as a stopover and base of operations. The English government eventually hired William Kidd to hunt down the pirates, but he himself turned pirate and seized a number of prizes. The scandal that the Kidd affair brought about in 1698 and 1699 led to the dissolution of all ties to Madagascar, and after the turn of the century many pirates were stranded on this remote island.

DOCUMENT 38

To the Arabian Sea with Captain Henry Avery (1695)[1]

Henry Avery disappeared in Ireland, but a few members of his crew were apprehended as they tried to disperse and rejoin established society. Some captives provided the authorities with comprehensive accounts of the voyage, probably in return for a promise not to be charged with any crime. William Philips' testimony shows that even then participants of the venture claimed not to have done anything illegal or wrong. Seizing valuables from a Muslim pilgrim fleet was not seen as a sin and therefore was not against the law. However, the real challenge for many pirates only emerged after they had robbed the desired booty and needed to find a way to continue their lives somewhere ashore where they could enjoy the ill-gotten wealth. The following narrative recounts the story of the voyage in remarkable detail.

---

1. Source: The National Archives, State Papers 63/358, fols. 127–32.

The voluntary confession and discovery of William Philips concerning the ship *Charles II*

In August 1693 (as I remember) I went on board the *Dove Galley*, Captain Humphreys Commander, in company with the *Charles II*, the *James*, and a pink bound for La Coruña and from thence to the Spanish West Indies.

At La Coruña the men demanded their pay which was to be paid by contract every six months, which not being paid them, and hearing the Spaniards and Irish designed to turn all the English on shore, and take their vessels from them, they were obliged to keep a very strict watch. Whereupon Henry Avery, master of the *Charles II*, went up and down from ship to ship and persuaded the men to come on board him, and he would carry them where they should get money enough. About 40 men came accordingly on board the said ship by night, upon which they cut the cables and loosed the sails having a fair wind to go out. The Spaniards hearing it, fired several shot from the town at us, but did no damage. When we came out of the reach of the castles and forts we gave the captain his pinnace which carried him and about seventeen more Spaniards and Irish ashore.

When we were thus got to sea after about three weeks sail finding ourselves short of provisions having but one barrel of beef and a small quantity of fish (but bread and water sufficient) we went to the Isle of May, being a Portuguese island near the coast of Guinea where we took in salt and about twenty bullocks. Here we met with three English ships, which we did no injury to but paid them for what we had of them, and seven of their men came voluntarily along with us.

From thence we went upon the coast of Guinea thinking to make a voyage there, but meeting with no prize we went away for Príncipe, being another island belonging to the Portuguese near the [Equatorial] Line, missing the island we fell in with an island called Fernando Poo, being about 150 leagues distant from Príncipe, sending our boat along shore to discover the inhabitants, and got some knowledge what the island was, they being unacquainted with trade ran away, but we finding a convenient place cleaned our ship, but in all this time we would not speak with one of the inhabitants.

From thence we steered again for Príncipe where we arrived (being about six months after our first departure from La Coruña) we took in here some rum and sugar and fresh provisions which we bought from the

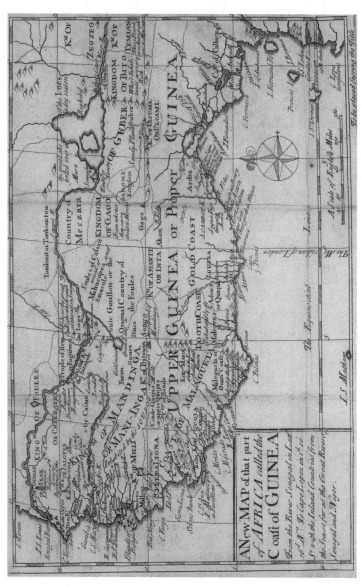

Map of West Africa showing Príncipe and Fernando Poo just north of the Equatorial Line and Cape Lopez in the bottom right corner. Source: John Carter Brown Library at Brown University.

inhabitants and paid them for. Here we met with two Danish men-of-war that had been redeeming a Danish factory on the coast of Guinea. We sent to them that if they would give us what provision we had occasion for and what money they had on board, their ship should go free, which they refusing telling us we were a thin schut and they did not fear us, we attacked them both together, and after an hour's dispute they yielded, upon which we took from them about 50 tons of brandy, and about 640 ounces of gold dust. We lost one man and killed four of them and one of the captains. We gave the men-of-war arms and provisions and a long-boat and set them ashore at Príncipe, 30 Dutch and Swedes took party with us and one of the chief merchants. We had a report at this time that we had a war with Denmark and they thought so too.

From thence we went back to Fernando Poo with the two Danes where, not knowing what to do with them, we burned the biggest and sunk the other at Cape Lopez. One of them had 26 guns and 80 men and was much bigger than us, the other 24 guns and 40 men. At this time our Ship, which was called *Fancy*, had 44 guns and but 80 men and was about 300 tons.

From thence we went for Cape Lopez about 100 leagues from Príncipe where we took in wax and honey in exchange for small arms. From thence we went for Annobón, a Portuguese island about 150 or 200 leagues distant from Cape Lopez (being about a month after our departure from Príncipe). Here we took in more water and oranges and about 50 hogs, which we paid for part money, part small arms.

From thence we sailed away for Madagascar in the East Indies. We arrived there in twelve weeks or thereabouts. There we bought about 100 bullocks for powder and small arms. After about a month stay we sailed for Anjouan, an English island being about 300 leagues where we arrived in about fourteen days. There we bought some hogs and paid for them. During our stay there three East India ships came in sight, upon which we made up to them under English colors, and finding them to be English we made the best of our way to the Red Sea.

In about three weeks we made the Babs key, which is the mouth of the Red Sea, before we arrived there we met two sail, which came up with us and proved to be upon the same account. We ordered them on board us. Captain Faro (who landed in the ship at Dunfanaghy) commanding one called the old barque and one Captain Want the other. The vessel being his own, called the Spanish bottom. They gave us two barrels of flour, and desired to go share and share with us, they were both but small vessels of 80 and 90 tons and about 60 men each. (They told us two more upon the same account were at Madagascar coming for these seas, one a brigantine Captain Meeze commander living in Rhode Island near New England. The other a vessel of about 100 tons Captain Wake called the new barque.) We sailed all night together and being bad weather lost one another and one ship lost her fore topmast, when we came to Babs key as aforesaid we found Captain Faro there, we asking him for his consort he said she was a bad sailor and he feared she could not get up. There we got a new top mast up and the Spanish bottom coming up told us she met with a Frenchman's small junk upon the same account with about 22 men. They were almost starved in the seas, and the Spanish bottom took them on board, and at Babs key we took them on board having more room. About three days after came up the new barque and the brigantine and a sloop, one Captain Tew, which Faro had told us of when being five of us together and a sloop we agreed on and signed articles to share and share alike.

During our stay here we sent a pinnace to Mocha being about 25 leagues distant to see what ships they could see there. At their return they told us there were about 40 sail, which we knew by a prisoner as well as by their seeing them in harbour. We asked the prisoner what ships they were and what money they had, he told us six sail of them were Jeddah ships and very rich.

We waited at Babs key 14 days before they came down, yet they escaped up in the night. The next day we took a small junk, which told us they were all gone. We made what haste we could after them. Our vessel being the best sailor we took the brigantine in tow. Captain Faro being a good sailor kept us company. We sunk the Spanish bottom and took the men on board us and the brigantine, the other two we left behind making after us. We sailed thus fourteen days and got before them, then stayed for them, and met with a ship of six guns which we took without resistance. She had a pretty quantity of silver and gold on board, we took her within ten leagues of where we have an English factory. He told us the Jeddah ships were all gone another way, only the admiral of Mecca, a very rich ship, was still behind. The next morning we saw a sail which we took to be the new barque, standing up to her a prisoner we had on board told us it was the admiral of Mecca, a ship of 70 guns and 700 men. Our vessel agreed to fight her with guns, and the brigantine and Faro were to board her, but they seeing her so big a ship durst not come near her (this was in about August 1695). When we came within shot she fired two chase guns of 18 pounders at us. They grazed our mizzenmast but did us no damage. We not intending to fire at them till we came on board and they fired the first broad side at us and overshot us being so large a ship, upon which we gave them eleven broad sides in all and boarded her, they then immediately surrendered, so we were masters of her in about two hours. They fired very warmly upon us all the while and threw fireworks into us to set our sails etc. on fire, but we lost never a man only one wounded in boarding. When we were on board they being all run into the hold, we called them up and gave them good quarter. We asked the captain what money he had on board. He told us he had one basket of about 2,000 pounds sterling that belonged to him, the rest belonged to Turkish merchants, which we found in the hold in baskets. There might be in the whole about 150,000 pounds sterling.

After two days we gave them the ship again taking the money out and we sailed all four together to Rajapur about 30 leagues from   where we have an English factory. There we watered and shared the money. We gave Captain Wake no share not being there and having taken a vessel by the way and shared about 100 pounds sterling a man. Faro in the old barque and four of his men we gave shares to being concerned in taking the first ship. The brigantine, Captain Meeze, showing a great readiness to assist us in the fight shared with us. Captain Want being in the brigantine after his own vessel, who the men turned out for a coward, and they are gone for the Gulf of Persia to make a voyage there. There were about 160 shares at 700 pounds sterling a piece or thereabouts, but it was not very equally divided. The brigantine and we sailed together toward Madagascar. In the way our men desiring to change their silver for the gold the brigantine's men clipped the gold before they exchanged with us. We sent for Captain Meeze on board and commanded all their money on board, and took it from them, but we gave them 2,000 pounds sterling among them and a small cable and anchor and they told us they would go for Madagascar and if they could get men go to sea again, if not they would load negroes there and so come for Rhode Island to which Captain Meeze belonged, and we have heard no more of her.

Wake told us he would go to St. Mary's in Madagascar expecting to meet a ship there of force of 22 guns, which he designed to buy and so go into the seas again, we heard no further of him but that the ship he expected did go and that she was built somewhere in New England on purpose.

Tew thinking to go to Madagascar fell in with an island called Don Mascareen belonging to the French, and in about 50 leagues from

Madagascar. Having 22 Frenchmen on board we sent some of them and some English to the factory to know if they would let us victual there, upon which the governor of the island came on board and entertained us very kindly. We bought 80 bullocks of him and salted them there, going ashore every day and being well treated by the inhabitants. The Frenchmen on board us would have persuaded us to have gone to Martinique and to have broken up there, which we would not consent to. So they would not go farther with us and persuaded 15 or 16 of our men to stay with them, designing to buy a small vessel that was building there and to go into the seas again.

Having cleared our ship we came away for the West Indies designing for New Providence where arriving within six leagues we sent a letter to Colonel Trott, the governor, and three men, Hollingsworth, Clinton and Adams by name, Captain Avery read the letter to us which was to this effect: That we were soldiers of fortune and had done no Christian nation any damage and were the King's subjects and to know whether he would entertain us, we sent a present of 500 pounds sterling with the letter. Adams came back in the governor's own sloop with some gentlemen of the island and brought us from the governor a cask of wine, a hogshead of beer and a cask of sugar, and told us we should be very welcome, whereupon we weighed anchor for [New] Providence where coming we fired all our guns and the governor answered us gun for gun. So the captain went ashore and some other officers and delivered the vessel to the governor to take care of her for the owners in England when all the men were gone ashore he sent some negroes and others to look after her, who being careless suffered the ship to run ashore where she was staved, which we supposed was done on purpose. We having first taken out the rigging and some of the guns, and we took the rest up before we came away. Whereupon Captain Avery, who now goes by the name of Captain Henry Bridgeman, bought a sloop which came to Dunfanaghy, Captain Faro commander.

Dublin, 8th August 1696
William Phillips

DOCUMENT 39

An Indian View of Avery's Attack on the *Ganj-i Sawai* (1695)[2]

The large prize that the pirate fleet seized was the Ganj-i Sawai, *which belonged to Abdul Ghafur, a prominent Gujarati merchant. As soon as the ship limped into Surat, rumors about the looting and killing of the pilgrims spread through the country. Angry crowds besieged the trading posts of the English East India Company, and commerce came to a standstill. Negotiations about reparations and future protection of Indian shipping ensued in the company headquarters in Bombay. One witness to the negotiations, Khafi Khan, who is described as a historian, left an account about this episode. It is one of the few surviving sources that mention sexual violence against women.*

The royal ship called the *Ganj-i Sawai*, than which there was no larger in the port of Surat, used to sail every year for the House of God (at Mecca). It was now bringing back to Surat 52 lacs of rupees in silver and gold, the produce of the sale of Indian goods at Mocha and Jedda. The captain of this ship was Ibrahim Khan. There were 80 guns and 400 muskets on board, besides other implements of war. It had come within eight or nine days of Surat, when an English ship came in sight, of much smaller size, and not having a third or fourth part of the armament of the *Ganj-i Sawai*. When it came within gun-shot, a gun was fired at it from the royal ship. By ill luck, the gun burst and three or four men were killed by its fragments. About the same time, a shot from the enemy struck and damaged the mainmast, on which the safety of the vessel depends. The Englishmen perceived this, and being encouraged by it, bore down to attack, and drawing their swords, jumped on board of their opponent. The Christians are not bold in the use of the sword, and there were so many weapons on board the royal vessel that if the captain had made any resistance, they must have been defeated. But as soon as the English began to board, Ibrahim Khan ran down into the hold.

---

2. Source: J. N. Das Gupta, *India in the Seventeenth Century as Depicted by European Travelers* (Calcutta: University of Calcutta, 1916), appendix A, 233–38.

The enemy soon became perfect masters of the ship. They transferred the treasure and many prisoners to their own ship. When they had laden their ship, they brought the royal ship to shore near one of their settlements, and busied themselves for a week searching plunder, stripping the men, and dishonoring the women, both old and young. They then left the ship, carrying off the men. Several honorable women, when they found an opportunity, threw themselves into the sea, to preserve their chastity, and some others killed themselves with daggers.

DOCUMENT 40

Adam Baldridge Chronicles the Dealings of Pirates in Madagascar (1699)[3]

During the 1690s the tiny island St. Mary's, located off the northeast coast of Madagascar, became a base of operations for pirates and slave traders. Adam Baldridge, a resident trader from New York, provided his lawless visitors with provisions and supplies in exchange for plunder. The establishment of the trading post provided pirates in the Indian Ocean with a harbor where they could call at between cruises and thus prolong their stay in the region. As his own account illustrates, Baldridge served as an intercultural broker connecting different branches of the pirate trade. Every business opportunity was explored and exploited. This document not only illustrates how pirates were driven by the desire to strike it rich, but they often met with failure and did not hesitate to prey upon each other. It seems reasonable to assume that some merchants in the American colonies made huge profits while the pirates risked, and sometimes lost, their lives.

July the 17th 1690 I, Adam Baldridge, arrived at the Island of St. Mary's in the ship *Fortune*, Richard Conyers commander, and on the 7th of January 1691 I left the ship being minded to settle among the negroes at St. Mary's with two men more, but the ship went to Port Dolphin and was cast away, April the 15th 1691, and half the men drowned and half saved

---

3. Source: The National Archives, Colonial Office 5/1042, fols. 212–14.

their lives and got ashore, but I continued with the negroes at St. Mary's and went to war with them. Before my going to war, one of the men died that went ashore with me and the other being discouraged went on board again, and none continued with me but my prentice John King. March the 9th they sailed for Bonavola on Madagascar, 16 leagues from St. Mary's, where they stopped to take in rice. After I went to war, six men more left the ship, whereof two of them died about three weeks after they went ashore and the rest died since. In May 1691 I returned from war

Map of Madagascar with St. Mary's island in the northeast and the major ports of call, St. Augustin and Port Dolphin, in the southwest and southeast, respectively. John Carter Brown Library at Brown University.

and brought 70 head of cattle and some slaves. Then I had a house built and settled upon St. Mary's, where great store of negroes resorted to me from the island Madagascar and settled the island St. Mary's, where I lived quietly with them, helping them to redeem their wives and children that were taken before my coming to St. Mary's by other negroes to the northward of us about 60 leagues.

October 13, 1691. Arrived the *Batchelor's Delight*, Captain George Raynor commander, burden 180 tons or thereabouts, 14 guns, 70 or 80 men, that had made a voyage into the Red Sea and taken a ship belonging to the Moors, as the men did report, where they took as much money as made the whole share run about 1,100 pounds sterling a man. They careened at St. Mary's, and while they careened I supplied them with cattle for their present spending, and they gave me for my cattle a quantity of beads, five great guns for a fortification, some powder and shot, six barrels of flour, [and] about 70 bars of iron. The ship belonged to Jamaica and set sail from St. Mary's November the 4th 1691, bound for Port Dolphin on Madagascar to take in their provisions, and December '91 they set sail from Port Dolphin bound for America, where I have heard since they arrived at Carolina and complied with the owners, giving them for ruin of the ship 3,000 pounds, as I have heard since.

October 14th 1692. Arrived the *Nassau*, Captain Edward Coates commander, burden 170 ton or thereabouts, 16 guns, 70 men, whereof about 30 of the men stayed at Madagascar, being most of them concerned in taking the hack boat at the Isle of May, Colonel Shrymton owner of the said hack boat was lost at St. Augustin. Captain Coates careened at St. Mary's, and whilst careening I supplied them with cattle for their present spending, and the negroes with fowls, rice and yams. For the cattle I had two chests and one jar of powder, six great guns and a quantity of great shot, some spikes and nails, five bolts of [canvas] duck and some twine, a hogshead of flour, the ship most of her belonged to the company, as they said Captain Coates set sail from St. Mary's in November '92 bound for Port Dolphin on Madagascar, and victualed there and in December set sail for New York. Captain Coates made about 500 pounds steling a man in the Red Sea.

August 7th 1693. Arrived the ship *Charles*, John Churcher master, from New York, Mr. Frederik Philipse owner, sent to bring me several sorts of goods. She had two cargoes in her, one consigned to said master to dispose of, and one to me, containing as follows: 44 pair of shoes and pumps, 6 dozen [pair] of worsted [wool] and thread stockings, 3 dozen of speckled shirts and breeches, 12 hats, some carpenters' tools, 5 barrels of rum, four quarter casks of Madeira wine, ten cases of spirits, two old stills full of holes, one worme [auger], two grindstones, two cross saws and one whip saw, three jars of oil, two small iron pots, three barrels of cannon powder, some books, catechisms, primers and horn books, two bibles, some garden seeds, three dozen of hoes, and I returned for the said goods 1,100 pieces of eight and dollars, 34 slaves, 15 head of cattle, 57 bars of iron. October the 5th he set sail from St. Mary's, after having sold part of his cargo to the white men upon Madagascar, to Mauratan to take in slaves.

October 19, 1693. Arrived the ship *Amity*, Captain Thomas Tew commander, burden 70 tons, 8 guns, 60 men, having taken a ship in the Red Sea that did belong to the Moors, as the men did report, they took as much money in her as made the whole share run 1,200 pounds sterling a man. They careened at St. Mary's and had some cattle from me, but for their victualing and sea store they bought from the negroes. I sold Captain Tew and his company some of the goods brought in the *Charles* from New York. The sloop belonged most of her to Bermuda. Captain Tew set sail from St. Mary's December the 23d 1693, bound for America.

August 1695. Arrived the *Charming Mary* from Barbados, Captain Richard Glover commander, Mr. John Beckford merchant and part owner, the most of the ship belonged to Barbados, the owners Colonel Russel, Judge Coates, and the Nisames [?]. She was burden about 200 tons, 16 guns, 80 men. She had several sort of goods on board. I bought the most of them. She careened at St. Mary's and in October she set sail from St. Mary's for Madagascar to take rice and slaves.

August 1695. Arrived the ship *Catherine* from New York, Captain Thomas Mostyn commander and supercargo, Mr. Frederick Philipse owner, the ship burden about 160 tons, no guns, near 20 men. She had several sorts of goods in her. She sold the most to the white men upon Madagascar, where he had careened. He set sail from St. Mary's for Mauratan on Madagascar to take in his rice and slaves.

December 7th 1695. Arrived the ship *Susanna*, Captain Thomas Wake commander, burden about 100 tons, 10 guns, 70 men. They fitted out from Boston and Rhode Island and had been in the Red Sea, but made no voyage by reason they missed the Moors' fleet. They careened at St. Mary's and I sold them part of the goods bought of Mr. John Beckford out of the *Charming Mary* and spared them some cattle, but for the most part they were supplied by the negroes. They stayed at St. Mary's until the middle of April, where the captain and master and most of his men died. The rest of the men that were left alive after the sickness carried the ship to St. Augustin, where they left her and went in [with] Captain Hore for the Red Sea.

December 11th 1695. Arrived the sloop *Amity*, having no captain, her former Captain Thomas Tew being killed by a great shot from a Moors' ship, John Yarland master, burden 70 ton, 8 guns, as before described, and about 60 men. They stayed but five days at St. Mary's and set sail to seek the *Charming Mary* and they met her at Mauratan on Madagascar and took her, giving Captain Glover the sloop to carry him and his men home and all that he had, keeping nothing but the ship. They made a new commander after they had taken the ship, one Captain Bobbington. After they had taken the ship they went into St. Augustin's Bay and there fitted the ship and went into the Indies to make a voyage and I have heard since that they were trapped and taken by the Moors.

December 29, 1695. Arrived a Moors' ship, taken by the *Resolution* and given to Captain Robert Glover and 24 of his men that was not willing to go a privateering upon the coasts of India, to carry them away. The company turned Captain Glover and these 24 men out of the ship, Captain Glover being part owner and commander of the same and confined prisoner by his company upon the coast of Guinea by reason he would not consent to go about the Cape of Good Hope into the Red Sea, the ship was old and would hardly swim with them to St. Mary's, when they arrived there they applied themselves to me. I maintained them in my house with provision until June that shipping arrived for to carry them home.

January 17th 1697. Arrived the brigantine *Amity* that was Captain Tew's sloop from Barbados and fitted into a brigantine by the owners of the *Charming Mary* at Barbados, Captain Richard Glover commander and supercargo, the brigantine described when a sloop. She was laden with several sorts of goods, part whereof I bought and part sold to the white men upon Madagascar, and part to Captain Hore and his company, the brigantine taken afterwards by the *Resolution* at St. Mary's.

February the 13th 1697. Arrived Captain John Hore's prize from the Gulf of Persia and three or four days after arrived Captain Hore in the *John and Rebecca*, burden about 180 tons, 20 guns, 100 men in ship and prize. The prize about 300 ton laden with calicoes. I sold some of the goods bought of Glover to Captain Hore and his company as likewise the white men that lived upon Madagascar and Captain Richard Glover.

June the   1697. Arrived the *Resolution*, Captain [Richard] Sievers commander, burden near 200 tons, 90 men, 20 guns, formerly the ship belonged to Captain Robert Glover, but the company took her from him and turned him and 24 more of his men out of her by reason they were not willing to go a privateering into the East Indies. They met with a monsoon at sea and lost all their masts and put into Madagascar about ten leagues to the northward of St. Mary's and there masted and fitted the ship, and while they lay there they took the brigantine *Amity* for her water casks, sails and rigging and masts, and turned the hull adrift upon a riff. Captain Glover promised to forgive them what was past if they would let him have his ship again and go with him to America, but they would not except he would go into the East Indies with them. September the 25th '97 they set sail to the Indies.

June 1697. Arrived the ship *Fortune* from New York, Captain Thomas Mostyn commander, and Robert Allison supercargo, the ship burden 150 tons or thereabouts, 8 guns, near 20 men, having several sorts of goods aboard, and sold to Captain Hore and company and to the white men upon Madagascar.

June   1697. Arrived a ship from New York, Captain Cornelius Jacobs commander and supercargo, Mr. Frederik Philipse owner, burden about 150 tons, 2 guns, near 20 men, having several sorts of goods on board, and sold to Captain Hore and his company and to the white men on Madagascar, and four barrels of tar to me.

July the 1st 1697. Arrived the brigantine *Swift* from Boston, Mr. Andrew Knott master and John Johnson merchant and part owner, burden about 40 tons, 2 guns, 10 men, having several goods aboard. Some sold to Captain Hore and company the rest put ashore at St. Mary's and left there. A small time after her arrival I bought three quarters of her and careened and went out to seek a trade and to settle a foreign commerce and trade in several places on Madagascar. About eight or ten days after I went from St. Mary's the negroes killed about 30 white men upon Madagascar and St. Mary's and took all that they or I had. Captain Mostyn and Captain Jacobs and Captain Hore's ship and company being all there at the same time and set sail from St. Mary's October 1697 for Madagascar to take in there slaves and rice. Having made a firm commerce with the negroes on

Madagascar, at my return I met with Captain Mostyn at sea, 60 leagues off St. Mary's, he acquainted me with the negroes' rising and killing the white men. He persuaded me to return back with him and not proceed any farther, for there was no safe going to St. Mary's, all my men being sick. After good consideration we agreed to return and go for America.

The above-mentioned men that were killed by the natives were most of them privateers that had been in the Red Sea and took several ships there. They were chiefly the occasion of the natives' rising, by their abusing of the natives and taking their cattle from them, and were most of them to the best of my knowledge men that came in several ships, as Captain Raynor, Captain Coates, Captain Tew, Captain Hore, and the *Resolution* and Captain Stevens.

5th of May 1699
Adam Baldridge

DOCUMENT 41

The Last Will of a Dying Pirate (1698)[4]

In December 1699 the authorities in the Dutch colony at the Cape of Good Hope seized the Margaret, a trading vessel bound for New York. The vessel had been in Madagascar to supply the pirates with necessities, and on its way back had loaded a cargo of slaves and pirate booty. On board were also a few retired pirates as well as letters and other paperwork connected to their activities. Among the documents was the last will of Joseph Jones, who had probably succumbed to a tropical disease. Like so many other pirates, he owned little. He was just a poor wretch who, affected by gold fever, probably tried to make the best of difficult circumstances. Piracy produced few winners and many losers. The will is particularly interesting because it shows that even in Madagascar, far away from the colonized world with all its norms, pirates followed established legal and religious conventions.

---

4. Source: The National Archives, High Court of Admiralty 1/98, fol. 108.

In the Name of God Amen ~

This ninth day of May in the year of our Lord God 1698 I, Joseph Jones, being very sick and weak of body, but of perfect mind memory thanks be given to God. I do make and ordain this my last will testament in manner and form following, that is to say first and chiefly I give my soul into the hands of Almighty God who gave it me and my body I commend to the earth to be buried in Christian burial at the discretion of executors hereafter named, nothing doubting but at the general resurrection I shall receive the same again by the mighty power of God, as touching my world by estate and affairs which it has pleased God to bless me I give devise and bequeath and dispose the same in manner and form following viz. I give devise and bequeath unto Francis Reed and John Bevis my full and whole executors my guns, pistols, ammunition, cartouche boxes, all my wearing apparel with my shares of the ship and a quarter part of part of what prise purchase or plunder shall be due to me from Jonathan Greene according to contract; Item I give devise and bequeath unto Michael Hicks one piece of gold Item I give devise and bequeath to Barrington Webb one piece of gold so this being my last will and given under my hand seal the day [and] year above written

Signed, sealed and	the mark
delivered in presence of us	of Joseph + Jones
John Watson	
Michael Hicks	

QUESTIONS TO CONSIDER FOR SECTION VII:

What made the Indian Ocean seem like a prime hunting ground for pirates?

What is the connection between piracy and the slave trade?

What were the obstacles to the creation of a lasting pirate culture here?

How did Indian Ocean raiding lead to the war against the pirates?

SECTION VIII: THE GOLDEN AGE OF PIRACY

The period between 1716 and 1726 is sometimes referred to as the Golden Age of Piracy. A dramatic upsurge of piracy began after the shipwreck of a Spanish silver fleet off Florida's east coast in August 1715. Within a few months hundreds of treasure hunters sailed to the site to loot the wrecks or rob silver and gold from the salvagers. It was not long before predatory activities expanded all over the Caribbean and the North Atlantic. During this period several thousand pirates roamed the seas and caused enormous damage to overseas trade of all nations. In the latter half of 1718 a notable shift occurred when a British force seized control of the Bahamas, the base of numerous raiders, and Edward Thatch, better known as Blackbeard, was killed in a fierce battle. In the following years many pirates sailed to the west coast of Africa and the South Atlantic, but the Caribbean remained the main theater of operations. Without access to safe havens, their days were numbered. Much of what we know about these criminals derives from *A General History of the Most Notorious Pyrates*, first published in 1724 at a time when the last desperados fought for survival. However, this often-cited book is riddled with exaggerations, misunderstandings, and factual errors and cannot be considered a reliable source.

DOCUMENT 42

Henry Bostock Encounters Blackbeard (1717)[1]

In late 1717 Edward Thatch, a.k.a. Blackbeard, emerged as the most famous pirate active in American waters. Like many of his fellow raiders, he initially used the Bahamas as a base of operations but quickly expanded predatory activities into the Caribbean and the North Atlantic. He then accepted the amnesty in North Carolina yet continued to seize shipping, including British merchant vessels. A series of brief articles in the first colonial newspaper,

---

1. Source: The National Archives, Colonial Office 152/12, fols. 219–20.

The *Boston News-Letter*, *told the stories of sailors who had been captured by Blackbeard. These reports transformed him into a legend. However, there are also a few more comprehensive eyewitness accounts, including the following one, which shows that force was usually not needed to seize one trading vessel after the other.*

The deposition of Henry Bostock, mariner

This deponent being duly sworn on the Holy Gospel says he was on the sloop *Margaret* of this island [St. Christopher] whereof he was master, he on the 5th day of this instant December at break of day turning up from Puerto Rico met about ten leagues to the westward of Crab Island a large ship and a sloop. The ship fired a smalls arm at him and then hailed him ordering him to come on board, which he with two of his men did in his canoe. Being conducted to the quarter deck to the person that we called the captain by the name (as he thinks) of Captain Tach, he asked the deponent what he had on board, to which this deponent answered he had cattle and hogs, then the said Captain Tach ordered his own boat to be hoisted out to go on board and fetch them, which they did (they were four beeves and about 35 hogs), they took from him beside two thirds of a barrel of gunpowder, five small arms, two cutlasses, his books and instruments, and some linen. This deponent declares the ship to be, as he thinks, Dutch built, was a French Guineaman (he heard on board) that she had then 36 guns mounted, that she was very full of men he believes 300 that they told him they had taken her about six or seven weeks before, that they did not seem to want provisions. That they kept him on board about eight hours, did not abuse him or any of his men, except the forcing of two of [them] to stay with them, whose names were Edward Salter, a cooper, formerly sailed with Captain George Moutton, and Martin Fowler. But one other man by name Robert Bibby, a Liverpool man, voluntarily took on with them. That he saw a great deal of plate on board of them, tankards, cups, etc. particularly one of his men took notice of a very fine cup, which they told him they had taken out of one Captain Taylor, whom they had taken going from Barbados to Jamaica, which Captain Taylor they very much abused, and, as he this deponent hears, burned his ship that they told this deponent that they had burned several vessels, among them two or three belonging to these islands, particularly the day before they had burned a sloop belonging to Antigua, one McGill owner, they claimed they had met with the men-of-war on this station, but said they had no business with her, but if she had chased them they would have kept their way. This deponent further says that he told them an act of grace was expected out for them but they seemed to slight it. This deponent says the captain was a tall spare man with a very black beard, which he wore very long. That among the men one Joe, a nephew to Doctor Rowland of this island, that sailed in Captain Joseph Wood from this island to London about three years ago, made himself known to this deponent enquiring after his said uncle etc. They asked this deponent whether there were any more traders on the Puerto Rico coast, which he this deponent would not give them an account of, but his men owned to them that there were two traders on the coast, one a French sloop and the other a Dane from St. Thomas. That whilst he was on board they ordered their consort, the sloop (on board of which he heard there were about 70 men) to make sail and chase along shore to look for these traders. This deponent says that by all he could guess from their discourse they intended for Samana Bay in Hispaniola to careen, and thence to lie in wait for the Spanish armada that they expected would immediately after Christmas come out of Havana for Hispaniola and Puerto Rico with the money to pay the garrisons, this they declared to him the captain saying they think we are gone but we will soon be on the backs of them unaware they having been heretofore on those coasts.

This deponent further says that they inquired of him where Captain Pinkethman was, that he told them he heard he was at St. Thomas with a commission from the King to go on the wrecks.

This deponent further says that among other riches he believed they had much gold dust on board for that an Indian and a negro belonging to Bermuda (as this defendant was informed at Tortola and by the above-said Robert McGill) having got from them at St. Croix, got with the said McGill's men on board a Danish sloop, and in her to Tortola. That one George Hanns, an Englishman formerly belonging to this island, was master of the said Danish sloop, who when he had the said negro and Indian on board, searched them and found on them as this deponent heard about fifteen ounces of gold dust, which this deponent was told at Tortola by one Henry Norton, the said Hanns, McGill, and a doctor on board shared between them. And further this deponent says not.

Henry Bostock

Sworn before me this 19th December 1717
William Mathew

DOCUMENT 43

Pillaging the Slave Trade (1719)[2]

After Woodes Rogers had taken control of the Bahamas, small groups of marauders left the islands and crossed the Atlantic to seek new hunting grounds on the coast of West Africa. There they seized numerous vessels. Many sailors voluntarily joined the pirates because conditions in the slave trade were atrocious and crew mortality was extremely high. Most slave vessels were captured before they loaded their human cargo. In a few cases when prizes had slaves on board the pirates left them untouched. The men were only interested in gold shipments. The following account summarizes events of the first half of 1719 that were reported in London with considerable delay.

An account of what vessels have been taken
by the pirates on the coast of Africa

One Captain [Howell] Davis, with nine men, went out from the island of [New] Providence in a longboat and took a sloop with nine hands, and all hands joining, came to the Cape Verde Islands, where they met with a Liverpool ship at the Isle of May and took her. She had on board about twenty men, all whom he forced with him, quitted his old sloop, and called the ship the *King James*. After that he went into Gambia River, where he took one French and two English ships, and getting most of their hands, mounted twenty guns. He then took Gambia Fort, brought the guns away and mounted the largest on board. As he came out of the river's mouth, he met a brigantine who fired at him and hoisted pirates' colors, and they doing the same, met and joined. This brigantine also began in the West Indies, and most of the men came from [New] Providence, who had been before pirates, but were pardoned. They both went into the River Sierra Leone, where they took the *Bird Galley*, Captain Snelgrave, and the *Sarah Galley* of London, shut up their decks and made pirates of them; the *Jacob and Jaell* of London, one Thompson commander, and a brigantine, one Bennet commander, both which they

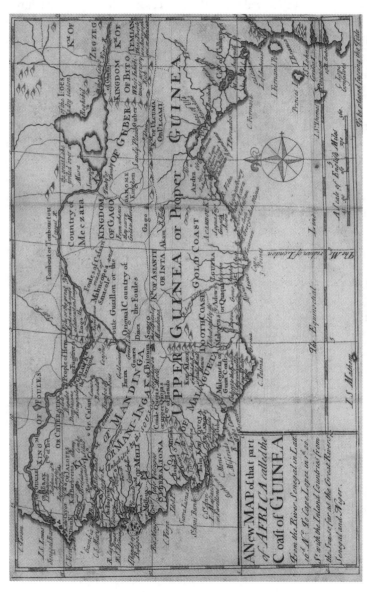

Map of West Africa showing Gambia Fort just below the western tip of the continent and the River Sierra Leone farther south. Anamaboe and Whydah are located on the Gold Coast. John Carter Brown Library at Brown University.

burned, the *Queen Elizabeth* and the *Dispatch*, both of London, and two more ships of Liverpool, the *Guineamen Sloop* and the *Elliot*, both of Barbados. They lay in the river about three weeks, in which time they fitted their ships and manned them, and took also the [Royal] African Company's fort and destroyed the place, and likewise did great damage to most of their ships, throwing overboard most of their cargoes, and then went out from Sierra Leone. These three pirates took a French ship, and threw all her cargo overboard, and a Liverpool snow, and a little after a snow belonging to Glasgow. Going farther along shore, took several canoes and killed the blacks. After they parted, the *Speakwell* and *Ormond* stayed behind, and the *King James* made all sail down the coast, and at Cape Appolonia met with a large Ostend ship. They both engaged, but the pirate soon took her; she had above twenty guns, they made her also a pirate, and threw all her cargo overboard, which some of them said cost above 8,000 pounds. Still going down, they took a longboat of the [Royal] African Company, and so came down to Anamaboe, where they took the *Royal Hind*, the *Hall*, and the *Prince*, all of London. They took a Dutch ship, and after plundering her discharged some of the men. The *King James*, and his consort, the other ship, as they made a pirate, called the *New King James*, with the *Prince*, went down toward Whydah, and a day after came down to the other two pirates, the *Speakwell* and *Ormond*, and took off the salt ponds the *Carteret* and a large ship of Barbados, and made her a pirate; she came down again, and retook the *Royal Hind* with what men was left on board, cut the rigging, and took his sails and all his stores, did what mischief they could, and left her a wreck. So went down and all met at the River Volta. Then went down to Whydah, where were three Frenchmen, three Portuguese, and the *Heroine Galley* of London, Captain Blincoe. Two of the French ships cut and ran away and got clear. Meanwhile they took the other and one of the Portuguese ships. They burned and made great destruction with the rest, for they wanted men and large ships to be stronger to go on the coast of Brazil, and then to the South Sea. They said they would do all mischief they could, for they knew they should have another pardon sent to call them in, and then they would go into [New] Providence.

DOCUMENT 44

A Skirmish with Bartholomew Roberts (1720)[3]

Between July 1719 and February 1722 a gang led by Bartholomew Roberts terrorized shipping almost all over the North Atlantic and the Caribbean. During this period he was said to have seized about 400 prizes, mostly small vessels. Few crews offered any resistance when they spotted the pirates' black flag. Why should sailors have risked their lives? Since the navy had almost no resources to confront seaborne robbers, merchants and colonial authorities did their best to get rid of the pirates who caused so much damage to their trade. In February 1720 news of Roberts sailing from Guyana toward the north reached Barbados. Local traders fitted out two vessels to chase down the notorious outlaw. This following account not only conveys the drama of the encounter with the pirates, but it also testifies to the difficulties in fighting them in the open sea.

Excerpt from the log of the *Somerset*

26 February [1720]

This 24 hours moderate gales and fair weather, at 10 of the clock in the morning saw two sail to windward and gave us chase, it being two pirate sloops, as soon as they came in gun shot, the biggest sloop fired a shot at us, and then another, and when they came in musket shot she fired another, then we hoisted our ensign and then up main sail and fore sail, the smallest sloop hoisted a broad black pennant with death's head etc. and ranged along our larboard side and called to us to strike, for they would give us quarter and then gave us a broadside with a continual fire of small arms and organs. Notwithstanding we lay all still in expectation they would board us, but on the contrary began their fire again, then put their helm hard a starboard and steered away. Then gave the word of command to let fly our pennant and jack and fired all our guns both below and above with a continual fire of small arms, which first action killed him two men

---

3. Source: The National Archives, Colonial Office 31/15, 1154–55.

in his boat, she being in tow, he then cut her away with three men in her, then we saw four of his men over board stopping his leaks, where we saw two of them wash away which in our opinion with the men in the tops supposed to have killed him above 35 men, he finding that we were so smart on him he made all the sail he could from us, and as for the small sloop, as soon as we began to engage she fired one gun and then made all the sail she could to the southward with his black flag flying, and as for Captain Greaves, he was no ways serviceable, for he was on our starboard quarter when we engaged the pirates on our larboard side nor neither did he discharge any of his guns or small arms at the time of action, but before we engaged I called to Captain Greaves to keep under my larboard quarter which he promised to do, but when he saw the pirate he got on my starboard quarter. And when we were engaged, Captain Greaves came under my stern, and close on board the pirate's stern, and ran between the said pirate and our ship, one of my officers put our helm hard a starboard to board the pirate, all our guns both great and small with pistols and cutlasses being ready to discharge, and board, but as much as I could do with my officers to prevent them from firing which if we had we must have done abundance of damage to Captain Greaves then calling to Captain Greaves and begging and praying that he would board the pirate, but he never made any assault or fired a gun until the pirate was almost out of gun shot, neither could we wear our ship, our running rigging, and being all shot about our ears we got all our sails set except our studding sails before Captain Greaves set his square sail and never made any more sail after the pirate than main sail jib and square sail, and towed his boat all the time and never fired but about four great shot at a distance, we gave chase until night to the northward, Captain Greaves' sloop sailed much better than the pirate, might have come up with him if he had made sail as he should have done, and we should not have been six minutes from them. At 7 of the clock I fired a gun to leave chase and stood away to the eastward and the pirate went northwest, and at eleven before noon I went on board Captain Greaves and inquiring what was the reason he did not board the pirate himself. All his officers did acknowledge that there was a great mistake in the man at helm, the second question I asked was to know why he did not give chase to the pirate and make more sail, their answer was that they had no topsail or spritsail, neither jib, halyards, nor had any arms loaded that time that we called them to board, Captain Greaves and company likewise informed me that when he went after the pirate he saw them throw overboard abundance of bread chests etc. and sawed down their gunwales.

DOCUMENT 45

The Legend of Anne Bonny and Mary Read (1720)[4]

Piracy is almost exclusively a male activity. On a few occasions, however, women have been present on pirate vessels. One such example occurred in the latter half of 1720 when a small group of outlaws led by John Rackam left the Bahamas to seek their fortune as raiders. Unfortunately, very little is known for fact about Anne Bonny and Mary Read, and the exact role they played on the high seas. One rare surviving account, along with a proclamation for their apprehension issued by Governor Rogers, was carried on a vessel to New England and published in the Boston Gazette. *Shortly thereafter the entire gang was captured and brought to Jamaica for trial. Both women pleaded to be spared the gallows because they were pregnant. While evidence suggests that Read died in prison in April 1721, Bonny disappeared in obscurity. The lack of specific information enabled the wider public to impose their own fantasies on these two poor women.*

New Providence, 4th September

Several pirates are on the coast of the Bahamas, among which is one Rackam who ran away with a sloop of six guns and took with him twelve men and two women. The governor of this place sent a sloop of 45 men after him. And on the second instant Doctor Rowan with his sloop and 54 hands, twelve guns, went out in order to suppress them, as did Captain Roach who arrived here from Barbados. The pirates swear destruction to all those who belong to this island.

---

4. Source: *The Boston Gazette*, October 17, 1720.

By his Excellency
Woodes Rogers, Esq. Governor of New Providence, &c.
A Proclamation

Whereas John Rackam, George Featherstone, John Davis, Andrew Gibson, John Howell, Noah Patrick   and two women, by name Anne Fulford alias Bonny and Mary Read, did on the 22nd of August last combine together to enter on board, take, steal, and run away with out of this Road of Providence, a certain sloop called the *William*, burthen about twelve tons, mounted with four great guns and a swivel one, also ammunition, sails, rigging, anchor, cables, and a canoe, owned by and belonging to Captain John Ham, and with the said sloop did proceed to commit robbery and piracy upon the boat and effects of James Gohier, Esq., master of a sloop riding at Berry Islands in his way from South Carolina to this port.

Wherefore these are to publish and make known to all persons whatsoever that the said John Rackam and his said company are hereby proclaimed pirates and enemies to the Crown of Great Britain and are to be so treated and deem'd by all his Majesty's subjects.

Given at Nassau, this 5th of September 1720

Sign'd Woodes Rogers

Anne Bonny and Mary Read, in *General History of the Pyrates* (London, 1724).
John Carter Brown Library at Brown University.

DOCUMENT 46

William Whelks Tells His Story (1723)[5]

In 1721 and 1722 the war against piracy was in full swing, and the number of raiders began to decline. Since few sailors volunteered to join pirate crews, many able men were pressed into service. The following story was told by a sailor who was forced on Thomas Anstis' vessel, presumably because of his navigational skills. Anstis had been part of Bartholomew Roberts' gang, but, in April 1721 when the company took course for Africa, he decided to stay in American waters and seek a way to return to mainstream society. However, there was no safe haven anymore, and rumors of a renewed amnesty proved to be elusive. This narrative provides an insight into the internal structure of a pirate gang at this difficult stage when frustration grew and tensions ran high. Attached to the narrative is a version of the pirate articles reflecting the most important issues the crews were dealing with when they roamed the Caribbean in the early 1720s.

The information of William Whelks of Minhead in the County [Somerset], mariner, taken upon oath before me, William Blake, Esq. one of His Majesties Justices of the Peace for this County, this 22th day of April Anno Domini 1723

This informant upon his oath says that in April 1721 he set sail from Bristol in the *Hamilton* frigate, Joseph Smith master and himself second mate, bound for Jamaica, that on the 22nd day of June the same year he was taken by the *Good Fortune* brigantine, a pirate ship about fifteen leagues to the westward of Cape Cruz by Thomas Anstis master and that he was detained on board the said ship by force by the said master for the space of twenty months and compelled to sign their articles and that during that time the said Thomas Anstis took divers ships both French, Dutch, English, and Spanish and plundered them of whatever he found necessary for their use. Some of whom after they had put the men on shore they burned or sunk. This informant further says that there was on board the said pirate ship about 80 white men and about 20 black

---

5. Source: The National Archives, Admiralty 1/4104, no. 75.

and that also this informant with two other men of the crew endeavored to make their escape from the said Thomas Anstis in the island of Tobago but was seized again by some of their crew and carried onboard the said pirate ship again and tried by their jury for desertion, for which they were severely whipped and this informant upon his oath further says that in January last (to the best of his memory) they took a Spanish sloop about 50 tons and carried her to Tobago aforesaid landing her crew there and put on board a sufficient number to sail her, of their own crew at which time the said pirate ship commanded by Anstis aforesaid was careening, their guns out which this informant observing, he with Joshua Underwood, Daniel Gleddon, William Simner, Zacharias Knowles, Stephen Weston, John Hammons, Peter Miller, Bridgstock Weaver, John Barker, Nathan Burd, and John Oram thought it a proper time to make their escape from him and accordingly seized the said Spanish prize and brought her to England under the command of Joshua Underwood aforesaid, and arriving at Padstow in Cornwall, he this deponent with Daniel Gleddon, William Simner, and John Oram aforesaid were put on shore near Padstow aforesaid when the said Joshua Underwood told this informant that he intended to be around for the other channel, this informant also says that at their leaving the said pirate ship they shared about twenty pounds apiece more or less, how the said Spanish sloop came to be foundered after they were on shore this informant knows not.

William Whelks

Articles made on board the *Good Fortune*

1st: That the captain shall have one full share as the rest of the company the master, gunner, carpenter, and boatswain the same.

2nd: If any man should disobey any lawful command of the commanding officers shall suffer punishment the company and captain shall think fit.

3rd: If any person or persons should go on board of any prize and should break open any chest without the knowledge of the quartermaster shall suffer what punishment the company and captain shall think fit.

4th: If any person or persons shall be found guilty of thievery from another to the value of one piece of eight shall be marooned on an island with one bottle of powder, one bottle of water, and shot equivalent.

5th: If any person or persons should be found neglecting in keeping their arms clean [or] unfitting for an engagement shall lose his share or shares.

6th: If any person or persons should be found to snap their arms or cleaning in the hold shall suffer Moses Law that is 40 lacking one.

7th: If any person or persons shall be found backwards in the time of an engagement shall be marooned.

8th: If any person or persons shall be found to game on board this privateer of the value of one rial plate shall suffer Moses Law.

9th: If any person or persons shall go on board of a prize and meet with any gentlewoman or lady of honor and should force them against their will to lye with them shall suffer death.

10th: If any person or persons should lose a leg or a limb or a joint shall for a limb have 800 pieces of eight and for one joint 200.

11th: If any time we shall come in company with any other marooner and that shall offer to sign their articles without the consent of the company shall be marooned or run away shall receive the same.

12th: But if at any time we shall hear from England and have an account of an act of grace they that are a mind to receive it shall go with their money and goods and the rest have the privateer.

DOCUMENT 47

Walter Moor Sets the Record Straight (1724)[6]

In 1723 and 1724 the number of pirates dwindled considerably. Many were chased down by naval forces, and pirate trials became regular occurrences in maritime colonies. The remaining pirates in turn grew desperate and increasingly violent. The most notorious cutthroats were Edward Low, Francis Spriggs, and George Lowther, who had turned to piracy after a mutiny on the Royal African Company vessel Gambia Castle in 1721. For two years the men looted one vessel after the other. At the time when Wal-

6. Source: The National Archives, Colonial Office 152/14, fol. 289.

ter Moor encountered this gang in the Caribbean there were few islands and coastal stretches—mostly in the Spanish empire—left where outlaws could rest without alerting the authorities, and none of these places were anywhere near any source of wealth. Sheer survival was the paramount concern for these pirates. The rather unspectacular demise of Lowther and some of his crew is recounted in the following document.

St. Christopher's

Taken before His Excellency John Hart Esq. Captain General and Governour in Chief in and over all His Majesties Leeward Carribbee Islands in America and Vice Admiral of the same.

The deposition of Walter Moor, age about 32 years, master of the sloop *Eagle*, being duly sworn on the Holy Evangelists of almighty God deposes and says as follows viz. that upon proceeding upon a voyage in the sloop *Eagle* from this island of St. Christopher to the Spanish coast, made the island of Blanquilla in the latitude of twelve [degrees] being bound for Cumaná upon the Spanish continent of America. And at the said island of Blanquilla this deponent saw a sloop on the 15th day of October last, and knowing that island to be a place where traders do not commonly use, it being uninhabited, supposed the said sloop to be a pirate. And did find the said sloop just careened with her sails unbent and her great guns on shore so took that advantage to attack her before she could get in a readiness to attack the said sloop *Eagle*. And when this deponent came near the said sloop, he was obliged to hoist his colors and fire a gun at the head of the other sloop to oblige her to show her colors and she answered with hoisting a Saint George's flag at the topmast head, and fired at this deponent's sloop *Eagle*. And when they found this deponent with his crew was resolved to board the said sloop, they cut their cables and hauled their stern on shore, which obliged this deponent to come to an anchor athwart their hawse, where he engaged them until they called for quarter and struck. At which time George Lowther, who was the captain on board the said pirates, with about ten or twelve of his crew made their escape out of the cabin windows. And then this deponent got the sloop off and secured her and went on shore with 25 men where they remained five days and nights in pursuit of the said Lowther and company and could not retake more than five of them. And then proceeded with the said sloop and about 24 of the said pirates to Cumaná aforesaid. And when this deponent arrived there, he informed the governor that he had taken a pirate sloop, upon which the governor sent a guard on board the piratical sloop. And had the said sloop afterwards tried and condemned and then delivered her to the sloop *Eagle's* company that took her. And then the said governor sent a small sloop to the island of Blanquilla with about 25 hands in pursuit of the pirates that were left there, which crew took four of the said pirates with seven small arms or thereabouts, leaving behind them the captain, three men and a little boy, which they could not take. And three of the four they took were condemned for life to be galley slaves and the other to the castle of Araya. And this deponent was informed that George Lowther the captain of the said pirate sloop had shot himself on the said island of Blanquilla and was found dead with his pistol busted by his side. And this deponent further says that he has several times heard some of the said crew, since their being taken by him say that they were on board the ship *Gambia Castle*, when she first was runaway with from Gambia, but their names this deponent does not remember, but very well knows the persons by sight that expressed themselves after this manner.

Walter Moor

10 March [1724]

DOCUMENT 48

A Final Display of the Black Flag (1726)[7]

The last pirates of the early modern period that were active between 1724 and 1726 were few—probably not more than two hundred—but they caused quite some stir in the Atlantic world. This was largely due to the fact that an increasing number of weekly or bi-weekly papers in London, as well as the colonies, published all available information on their depredations. Newspaper reports about pirate trials and executions were important exercises in colonial authority, designed to build or rebuild trust in the rule of law, and boost morale in the war against piracy. It seems therefore reasonable to assume that not every detail in the

---

7. Source: *The Boston Gazette*, March 28, 1726.

following description is accurate. At this time legends emerged, and the pirate myths that were to play a significant role in popular culture were created.

Philadelphia, February 22 [1726]

We have advice from Barbados that the barbarous [Philip] Lyne, formerly consort to [Francis] Spriggs, the pirate, that he and his crew was taken and carried unto Curaçao. The way they went to be tried was thus, the commander went at the head, with about 20 other pirates, with their black silk flag before them, with the representation of a man in full proportion, with a cutlass in one hand, and a pistol in the other extended. As they were much wounded, and no care taken in dressing, they were very offensive, and stunk as they went along, particularly Lyne the commander. He had one eye shot out, which with part of his nose, hung down on his face. There was a master of a vessel retaken with them, whom Lyne had snapped his pistol at several times together, with an intent to shoot him through the head, but it missing fire so often, he threw it down on the deck, and swore he would not kill another man while he lived. One of the people immediately taking it up, fired it off at the first trial into the sea, and it was God's will to prevent him from breaking his oath by putting him into the way of the two sloops soon after. He confessed upon trial that he had killed 37 masters of vessels, besides foremastmen, during the time of his piracy.

QUESTIONS TO CONSIDER FOR SECTION VIII:

What do we learn of the "last" pirates' own motives from the various testimonies?

Who were their main victims and how did they respond?

How did the various sources describe these sea raiders on the eve of extinction?

What distinguishes them from the buccaneers and corsairs who came before?

GLOSSARY AND PLACE NAMES

almiranta	second-in-command ship in a Spanish fleet
Anamaboe	slave trading post in present-day Ghana
Anjouan	island in the Comoros
Annobón	small island in the Gulf of Guinea
Aquilon	French name for a northwesterly wind in the Caribbean
Araya	peninsula in the northeast of Venezuela
Armada de Barlovento	Spanish fleet for the protection of Caribbean shipping
arquebus	primitive matchlock gun
Badara	Vadakara, India
barque	two-masted sailing vessel
belly timber	food of all sorts
Berry Islands	chain of islands in the northwest of the Bahamas
Blanquilla	small island off the northeast coast of Venezuela
Bonavola	place of call on Madagascar's east coast
breaking bulk	removing loose cargo
brigantine	two-masted sailing vessel
calabash	bottle made from the shell of a calabash tree
Calicut	coastal town and center of spice trade in southwestern India
Callao	port of Lima
Cannanore	coastal town and center of spice trade in southwestern India
Caño	later named Isla de la Plata, off Ecuador
Cape Appolonia	southern point of West Africa
Cape Clare	Punta Mala, Panama?
Cape Cruz	western tip of Cuba
Cape Gracias a Dios	cape in the north of the Mosquito Coast near the border of Honduras and Nicaragua
Cape Lopez	cape on the southwest coast of Africa
Cape Pasado	cape in Ecuador
Cape of San Francisco	cape in Ecuador
Cape of the Plateforme	coastal stretch in the northwest of Hispaniola

Cape Tiburon	southwestern point of Hispaniola
capitana	leading ship in a Spanish fleet
careen	practice of hauling over vessels to clean the bottom
carrack	three- or four-masted vessels used in the sixteenth century
Cartagena	Caribbean port in Colombia
Cayo de Piedras	Cayo Piedra del Obispo, Cuba?
Chagre	river along the treasure route in central Panama
Chérrepe	small coastal town in the northwest of Peru
Cocinas	islands off the Belize coast
cocket	seal or seal permit
corselet	a piece of body armor covering the trunk
Crab Island	Vieques, island just east of Puerto Rico
culverin	cannon with long barrel
Cumaná	port town in the northeast of Venezuela
Darien	mountainous region in the far east of Panama
Don Mascareen	old name for present-day La Réunion
escudo	a Spanish gold coin weighing about 3.34g
fathom	a unit of length equal to six feet to measure depth of water
Fernando Poo	small island in the Gulf of Guinea
frigate	naval vessel with multiple masts
galley	long sailing vessel with oars to be rowed
galliot	small cargo vessel
Gambia Fort	small trading post in West Africa
Gelves	Djerba, Tunisia
Genoese	refers to Domingo Grillo and Ambrosio Lomelin who possessed the privilege to supply the Spanish colonies with slaves between 1662 and 1671
Golden Island	small island off the northeast coast of Panama
Gonaïves	settlement on Hispaniola's west coast
Granada	town near the western end of Lake Nicaragua
Grand Cayman	small island south of Cuba
Gulf of Saragua	bay that made up the west coast of Hispaniola
hack boat	boat used for maintenance duties
halberd	a combined spear and battle-ax

Huarmey	small coastal town in Peru
hulk	vessel without rigging
Isle of May	Maio, Cape Verde Islands
Isle of Plate	island off Ecuador's Pacific coast (see Caño)
jagher	small Dutch sailing vessel similar to a yacht
Jalteba	native village near Granada, Nicaragua
jib	triangular sail that sets ahead of the foremast
junk	Asian vessel with a flat bottom
King Golden Cap	legendary native leader who used to wear something like a crown
La Cantara	El Kantara, Djerba, Tunisia
lacs of rupees	Indian convention of grouping larger sums of money
Laguna de Términos	large lagoon in the southwest of the Yucatan Peninsula
league	three nautical miles
Lepanto	place in Greece
licenciate	Spanish man with law degree
Lida	probably referring to Ometepe, then known as Isla de Nicaragua
Livorno	port town on Italy's west coast
longboat	open boat to be rowed by eight or ten men
Lorenzo	Laurens de Graaf
Margarita	small island off Venezuela
marooner	outcast who roams in the wild
Matanzas	port in northern Cuba and name of a landing place on the northeast coast of Panama
mizzenmast	the mast aft of a ship's mainmast
Monkey Bay	wide bay on the southern Mosquito Coast
Moses Law	ancient method of punishment
Mosquitoes	Mosquito Coast
Nair	group of Indian Hindu castes
New Providence	island in the Bahamas
Nicoya	peninsula on Costa Rica's Pacific coast
Nombre de Dios	town on Panama's Caribbean coast
packet boat	large boat to carry mail and dispatches
Paita	port town in northwestern Peru

Paraíba	province in northeastern Brazil
patache	boat used for communication between vessels of a fleet
Petit-Goâve	harbor in the southwest of Hispaniola
piece of eight	Spanish silver coin worth one peso
pig of plate	silver ingot
pilot	person with local knowedge to natigate a vessel
pink	small vessel with a narrow stern
pinnace	boat used as a tender to a larger vessel
pirogue	dugout vessel with with one pointed and one flat end
pistole	gold coin used in Europe
Piura	town in the northwest of Peru
plate	uncoined silver, usually referring to silverware, cups, etc.
Point Cagway	port on the south coast of Jamaica, in 1660 renamed Port Royal
Port Dolphin	Fort Dauphin, an abandoned French settlement on the southeast coast of Madagascar
Portobelo	port on Panama's Caribbean coast
Príncipe	Portuguese trading post in the Gulf of Guinea
prize	seized vessel
Providence	small island off Nicaragua's Caribbean coast
Quibdó	town in western Colombia
Rajapur	trading post of the East India Company on India's west coast
Realejo	shipbuilding center on Nicaragua's Pacific coast
rial plate	silver piece of eight, or peso of eight reales (rials)
Río de la Hacha	modern Riohacha, Caribbean port in Colombia
River Andriel	river in the southeast of Panama
River Lagartos	river in the Yucatan Peninsula
River Suerre	river in Costa Rica
Roatán	small island off the coast of Honduras
rover	Dutch term for marauder
Sacrificio	small island near Veracruz
Salt Tortudos	small island off Venezuela
Samana Bay	bay on the northeast coast of Hispaniola
San Juan de Ulúa	fortification protecting the port of Veracruz
Santa Maura	Levkas, Greece

schut	small flat-bottomed boat
seraglio	women's living quarters in an Ottoman palace
ship	watercraft with three or more masts
sloop	single-masted sailing vessel
snow	square rigged vessel with two masts
Solentiname	islands in the southeast of Lake Nicaragua
South Sea	old term for the Pacific Ocean including parts of the South Atlantic
Spanish Main	north coast of South America plus Panama
spar	pole of wood used in the rigging to support the sail
squadron	portion of a naval fleet
St. Augustin	port of call in the southwest of Madagascar
St. Christopher	old name for St. Kitts
St. Croix	island in the Lesser Antilles
stanza	an arrangement of a certain number of lines
stern	back part of a vessel
stockades	wooden defense works; remains of El Real de Santa María, destroyed by natives in 1680
swivel gun	small cannon mounted on stand or fork
tankard	form of drinkware with single handle
Toa	Toa Bajo, Puerto Rico
Tobagilla	small island near Tobago
Tobago	island off northeastern Venezuela
Tortola	island in the Lesser Antilles
Troy-Point	Troia, Turkey
Trujillo	name of port towns in Honduras and Peru
Venta de Cruces	settlement on the Chagres River in Panama
vessel	watercraft with one or two masts
La Villa	small town on Panama's southeast coast
Villahermosa	town in Tabasco
Waggoner	collection of charts named after Lucas Janssen Waghenaer's 1584 atlas
Whydah	slave trading post in Benin
Zaña	small town in northern Peru

SELECT BIBLIOGRAPHY

Anderson, John L. "Piracy and World History: An Economic Perspective on Maritime Predation." *Journal of World History* 6 (1995): 175–99.

Andrews, Kenneth R. *The Spanish Caribbean: Trade and Plunder, 1530–1630*. New Haven: Yale University Press, 1978.

Antony, Robert. *Elusive Pirates, Pervasive Smugglers: Violence and Clandestine Trade in the Greater China Seas*. Hong Kong: Hong Kong University Press, 2010.

———. *Like Froth Floating on the Sea: The World of Pirates and Seafarers in Late Imperial South China*. Berkeley: University of California Press, 2003.

———. *Pirates in the Age of Sail*. New York: W. W. Norton, 2007.

Apestegui, Cruz. *Pirates of the Caribbean: Buccaneers, Privateers, Freebooters and Filibusters*. London: Conway, 2002.

Appleby, John C. *Under the Bloody Flag: Pirates in the Tudor Age*. Stroud: The History Press, 2009.

———. *Women and English Piracy, 1540–1720: Partners and Victims of Crime*. Woodbridge: Boydell Press, 2013.

Arnold, A. James. "From Piracy to Policy: Exquemelin's *Buccaneers* and Imperial Competition in America." *Review: Literature and Arts of the Americas* 40 (2007): 9–20.

Atauz, Ayse Devrim. *Eight Thousand Years of Maltese Maritime History: Trade, Piracy, and Naval Warfare in the Central Mediterranean*. Gainesville: University Press of Florida, 2008.

Baer, Joel H., ed. *British Piracy in the Golden Age: History and Interpretation, 1660–1730*. 4 vols. London: Pickering and Chatto, 2007.

———. *Pirates of the British Isles*. Stroud: Tempus, 2005.

Bahar, Matthew R. "People of the Dawn, People of the Door: Indian Pirates and the Violent Theft of an Atlantic World." *Journal of American History* 101 (2014): 401–26.

Battesti, Michèle, ed. *La piraterie au fil de l'histoire: un défi pour l'Etat*. Paris: Presses de l'Université Paris-Sorbonne, 2012.

Bawlf, Samuel. *The Secret Voyage of Sir Francis Drake, 1577–1580*. New York: Penguin, 2003.

Beal, Clifford. *Quelch's Gold*. Westport, CT: Praeger, 2007.

Bentley, Jerry, Renate Bridenthal, and Karen Wigen, eds. *Seascapes: Maritime Histories, Littoral Cultures, and Transoceanic Exchanges*. Honolulu: University of Hawai'i Press, 2007.

Benton, Lauren. "Legal Spaces of Empire: Piracy and the Origins of Ocean Regionalism." *Comparative Studies in Society and History* 47 (2005): 700–24.

———. *A Search for Sovereignty: Law and Geography in European Empires, 1400–1900*. New York: Cambridge University Press, 2010.

Berbouche, Alain. *Pirates, flibustiers et corsaires: le droit et les réalités de la guerre de Course*. Saint-Malo: Presses Galoné, 2010.

Bernal Ruiz, María del Pilar. *La toma del puerto de Guayaquil en 1687*. Sevilla: Escuela de Estudios Hispano-Americanos, 1979.

Bialuschewski, Arne. "Between Newfoundland and the Malacca Strait: A Survey of the Golden Age of Piracy, 1695–1725." *Mariner's Mirror* 90 (2004): 167–86.

———. "Black People under the Black Flag: Piracy and the Slave Trade on the West Coast of Africa, 1718–1723." *Slavery and Abolition* 29 (2008): 461–75.

———. "Jacobite Pirates?" *Histoire sociale/Social History* 44 (2011): 147–64.

———. "Pirates, Black Sailors, and Seafaring Slaves in the Anglo-Maritime World, 1716–1726." *Journal of Caribbean History* 45 (2011): 143–58.

———. "Pirates, Markets, and Imperial Authority: Economic Aspects of Maritime Depredations in the Atlantic World, 1716–1726." *Global Crime* 9 (2008): 52–65.

Blakemore, Richard J. "The Politics of Piracy in the British Atlantic, c. 1640–1649." *International Journal of Maritime History* 25 (2013): 159–72.

Blom, Hans, ed. *Property, Piracy and Punishment: Hugo Grotius on War and Booty in De Iure Praedae—Concepts and Contexts*. Leiden: Brill, 2009.

Bose, Sugata. *A Hundred Horizons: The Indian Ocean in the Age of Global Empire*. Cambridge, MA: Harvard University Press, 2006.

Boullosa, Carmen. *El médico de los piratas: Bucaneros y filibusteros en el Caribe*. Madrid: Siruela, 2002.

Bracewell, Catherine. *The Uskoks of Senj: Piracy, Banditry, and Holy War in the Sixteenth-Century Adriatic*. Ithaca: Cornell University Press, 2011.

Bradley, Peter T. *The Last Buccaneers in the South Sea, 1686–1695*. Morrisville, NC: Lulu, 2011.

———. *Spain and the Defence of Peru, 1579–1700: Royal Reluctance and Colonial Self-Reliance*. Morrisville, NC: Lulu, 2009.

———. *The Lure of Peru: Maritime Intrusion into the South Sea, 1598–1701*. New York: St. Martin's Press, 1989.

Britto García, Luis. *Demonios de mar: Piratas y corsarios en Venezuela, 1528–1727*. Caracas: Fundación Francisco Herrero Luque, 1998.

———. *Señores del Caribe: Indígenas, conquistadores y piratas en el mar colonial*. Caracas: Fundación Tradiciones Caraqueñas, 2001.

Burg, Barry R. *Sodomy and the Pirate Tradition: English Sea Rovers in the Seventeenth-Century Caribbean*. New York: New York University Press, 1984.

Burl, Aubrey. *Black Barty: The Real Pirate of the Caribbean.* Stroud: The History Press, 2005.

Butel, Paul. *Les Caraïbes au temps des flibustiers.* Paris: Aubier Montaigne, 1982.

Buti, Gilbert, and Philippe Hrodej, eds. *Dictionnaire des corsairs et des pirates.* Paris: CNRS, 2013.

Butler, Lindley S. *Pirates, Privateers, and Rebels of the Carolina Coast.* Chapel Hill: University of North Carolina Press, 2000.

Camus, Michel-Christian. *L'île de la Tortue au cœur de la flibuste caraïbe.* Paris: L'Harmattan, 1997.

———. "Une note critique à propos d'Exquemelin." *Revue française d'histoire d'Outre-mer* 77 (1990): 79–90.

Cheng Wei-Chung. *War, Trade and Piracy in the China Seas, 1622–1683.* Leiden: Brill, 2013.

Clifford, Barry, and Kenneth J. Kinkor, with Sharon Simpson. *Real Pirates: The Untold Story of the* Whydah *from Slave Ship to Pirate Ship.* Washington, DC: National Geographic, 2007.

Cordingly, David. *Pirate Hunter of the Caribbean: The Adventurous Life of Captain Woodes Rogers.* New York: Random House, 2011.

———. *Under the Black Flag: The Romance and Reality of Life among the Pirates.* New York: Random House, 1996.

Creighton, Margaret S., and Lisa Norling, eds. *Iron Men, Wooden Women: Gender and Seafaring in the Atlantic World, 1700–1920.* Baltimore: Johns Hopkins University Press, 1996.

Cromwell, Jesse. "Life on the Margins: (Ex)Pirates and Spanish Subjects on the Campeche Logwood Frontier, 1660–1716." *Itinerario* 33 (2009): 43–71.

Davies, Charles. *The Blood-Red Arab Flag: An Investigation into Qasimi Piracy, 1797–1820.* Exeter: University of Exeter Press, 1997.

Davis, Robert C. *Christian Slaves, Muslim Masters: White Slavery in the Mediterranean, the Barbary Coast, and Italy, 1500–1800.* New York: Palgrave Macmillan, 2003.

Donoso Bustamente, Sebastián I. *Los últimos piratas del Pacífico.* Quito: Planeta, 2014.

———. *Piratas en Guayaquil: Historia del asalto de 1687.* Quito: El Universo, 2006.

Earle, Peter. *The Pirate Wars.* London: Methuen, 2003.

———. *The Sack of Panamá: Sir Henry Morgan's Adventures on the Spanish Main.* New York: Viking Press, 1981.

———. *The Treasure of the* Concepción: *The Wreck of the Almiranta.* New York: Viking Press, 1980.

Exquemelin, Alexander O. *The Buccaneers of America.* Translated by Alexis Brown. New York: Dover, 2000.

———. *Histoire des aventuriers flibustiers*. Edited by Réal Ouellet. Paris: Presses de l'Université Paris-Sorbonne, 2005.

Feijoo, Ramiro. *Corsarios berberiscos: El reino corsario que provocó la guerra mas larga de la historia de España*. Madrid: Carroggio/Belaqva, 2003.

Flemming, Gregory N. *At the Point of a Cutlass: The Pirate Capture, Bold Escape, and Lonely Exile of Philip Ashton*. Lebanon, NH: ForeEdge, 2014.

Fox, Edward T. *King of the Pirates: The Swashbuckling Life of Henry Every*. Stroud: The History Press, 2008.

Friedman, Ellen G. *Spanish Captives in North Africa in the Early Modern Age*. Madison: University of Wisconsin Press, 1983.

Frohock, Richard. *Buccaneers and Privateers: The Story of the English Sea Rover, 1675–1725*. Newark: University of Delaware Press, 2012.

Galvin, Peter. *Patterns of Pillage: A Geography of Caribbean-based Piracy in Spanish America, 1536–1718*. New York: Peter Lang, 1999.

García de León, Antonio. *Vientos bucaneros: Piratas, corsarios y filibusteros en el Golfo de México*. Mexico City: Ediciones Era, 2013.

Gasser, Jacques. *Dictionnaire des flibustiers des Caraïbes: corsaires et pirates français au XVIIe siècle*. Les Sables d'Olonne: Editions de Beaupré, 2017.

Gerassi-Navarro, Nina. *Pirate Novels: Fictions of Nation Building in Spanish America*. Durham, NC: Duke University Press, 1999.

Gerhard, Peter. *Pirates of the West Coast of New Spain, 1575–1742*. Cleveland: Arthur H. Clark, 1960.

Gosse, Philip. *The History of Piracy*. London: Longmans, Green, 1932.

Govil, Aditi. "Mughal Perception of English Piracy: Khafi Khan's Account of the Plunder of *Ganj-i Sawai* and the Negotiations at Bombay, 1694." *Proceedings of the Indian History Congress* 61 (2000–2001): 407–12.

Graham, Eric J. *Seawolves: Piracy and the Scots*. Edinburgh: Birlinn, 2005.

Greene, Molly. *Catholic Pirates and Greek Merchants: A Maritime History of the Mediterranean*. Princeton: Princeton University Press, 2010.

Hahn, Steven C. "The Atlantic Odyssey of Richard Tookerman: Gentleman of South Carolina, Pirate of Jamaica, and Litigant before the King's Bench." *Early American Studies* 15 (2017): 539–90.

Hampden, John, ed. *Francis Drake, Privateer: Contemporary Narratives and Documents*. Tuscaloosa: University of Alabama Press, 1972.

Hanna, Mark. *Pirate Nests and the Rise of the British Empire, 1570–1740*. Chapel Hill: University of North Carolina Press, 2015.

———. "Well-Behaved Pirates Seldom Make History: A Reevaluation of English Piracy in the Golden Age." In *Governing the Sea in the Early Modern Era: Essays in Honor of Robert C. Ritchie*, edited by Peter C. Mancall and Carole Shammas. Los Angeles: USC-Huntington Library Press, 2015.

Haring, Clarence H. *The Buccaneers in the West Indies in the XVIIth Century*. London: Methuen, 1910.

Hawkins, Richard. *Voyage into the South Sea* [1622 facsimile ed.]. Amsterdam: Da Capo Press, 1968.

Head, David, ed. *The Golden Age of Piracy: The Rise, Fall, and Enduring Popularity of Piracy.* Athens, GA: University of Georgia Press, 2018.

Heers, Jacques. *The Barbary Corsairs: Warfare in the Mediterranean, 1480–1580.* London: Stackpole, 2003.

Heller-Rozan, Daniel. *The Enemy of All: Piracy and the Law of Nations.* New York: Zone Books, 2009.

Hoffman, Paul E. *The Spanish Crown and the Defense of the Caribbean, 1535–1585: Precedent, Patrimonialism, and Royal Parsimony.* Baton Rouge: Louisiana State University Press, 1980.

Horden, Peregrine, and Nicholas Purcell. *The Corrupting Sea: A Study of Mediterranean History.* New York: Oxford University Press, 2000.

Howse, Derek, and Norman Thrower. *A Buccaneer's Atlas: Basil Ringrose's South Sea Waggoner.* Berkeley: University of California Press, 1992.

Jaeger, Gérard. *Pirates, flibustiers et corsaires: histoire et légendes d'une société d'exception.* Avignon: Aubanel, 1987.

Jameson, J. Franklin, ed. *Privateering and Piracy in the Colonial Period: Illustrative Documents.* New York: Macmillan, 1923.

Jamieson, Alan G. *Lords of the Sea: A History of the Barbary Corsairs.* London: Reaktion Books, 2012.

Jármy Chapa, Martha de. *Un eslabón perdido en la historia: Piratería en el Caribe, siglos XVI y XVII.* Mexico City: Universidad Nacional Autónoma, 1983.

Johnson, Charles [pseud.]. *A General History of the Pyrates.* New York: Dover, 1999.

Jowitt, Claire. *The Culture of Piracy, 1580–1630: English Literature and Seaborne Crime.* Burlington, VT: Ashgate, 2010.

Juárez Moreno, Juan. *Corsarios y piratas en Veracruz y Campeche.* Sevilla: Escuela de Estudios Hispano-Americanos, 1972.

Kelsey, Harry. *Francis Drake: The Queen's Pirate.* New Haven: Yale University Press, 2000.

———. *Sir John Hawkins: The Queen's Slave Trader.* New Haven: Yale University Press, 2003.

Kempe, Michael. "Even the Remotest Corners of the World: Globalized Piracy and International Law, 1500–1900." *Journal of Global History* 5 (2010): 353–72.

———. *Fluch der Weltmeere: Piraterie, Völkerrecht und internationale Beziehungen, 1500–1900.* Frankfurt: Campus, 2010.

Knivet, Anthony. *The Admirable Adventures and Strange Fortunes of Master Anthony Knivet: An English Pirate in Sixteenth-Century Brazil.* Edited by Vivien Kogut Lessa de Sá. New York: Cambridge University Press, 2015.

Konstam, Angus. *Blackbeard: America's Most Notorious Pirate.* Hoboken, NJ: Wiley, 2006.

————. *The History of Pirates*. New York: Mercury Books, 2005.

————. *The World Atlas of Pirates*. New York: Lyons Press, 2009.

Kritzler, Edward. *Jewish Pirates of the Caribbean: How a Generation of Swashbuckling Jews Carved out an Empire in the New World*. New York: Anchor, 2009.

Labat, Jean-Baptiste. *The Memoirs of Pere Labat, 1693–1705*. London: Constable, 1931.

Lane, Kris. *Pillaging the Empire: Piracy on the High Seas, 1500–1750*. New York: Routledge, 2015.

————. "Punishing the Sea Wolf: Corsairs and Cannibals in the Early Modern Caribbean." *New West India Guide* 77 (2003): 201–20.

Lapouge, Gilles. *Les pirates: forbans, flibustiers, boucaniers et autres gueux de mer*. Paris: Hachette Illustrated, 2001.

Latimer, Jon. *Buccaneers of the Caribbean: How Piracy Forged an Empire*. Cambridge, MA: Harvard University Press, 2009.

Le Bris, Michel, ed. *L'aventure de la flibuste: actes du colloque de Brest*. Paris: Hoebeke, 2002.

Lécureur, Michel. *Corsaires et pirates de Normandie*. Paris: Magellan & Cie, 2011.

Leeson, Peter T. *The Invisible Hook: The Hidden Economics of Pirates*. Princeton: Princeton University Press, 2009.

————. "An-*arrgh*-chy: The Law and Economics of Pirate Organization." *Journal of Political Economy* 115 (2007): 1049–94.

Lincoln, Margarette. *British Pirates and Society, 1680–1730*. Farnham: Ashgate, 2014.

López Lázaro, Fabio. "Labour Disputes, Ethnic Quarrels, and Early Modern Piracy: A Mixed Hispano-Anglo-Dutch Squadron and the Causes of Captain Every's 1694 Mutiny." *International Journal of Maritime History* 22 (2010): 73–111.

————. *The Misfortunes of Alonso Ramírez: The True Adventures of a Spanish American with 17th-Century Pirates*. Austin: University of Texas Press, 2011.

López Pérez, Alessandro, and Mónica Pavía Pérez. *Malhechores de la mar: Corsarios, piratas, negreros, ragueros y contrabandistas*. La Habana: Ediciones Boloña, 2015.

López Zea, Leopoldo Daniel. *Piratas del Caribe y Mar del Sur en el siglo XVI*. Mexico City: Universidad Nacional Autónoma, 2003.

Lucena Salmoral, Manuel. *Piratas, bucaneros, filibusteros y corsarios en América: Perros, mendigos y otros malditos del mar*. Madrid: MAPFRE, 1992.

Lunsford, Virginia. *Piracy and Privateering in the Golden Age Netherlands*. London: Palgrave Macmillan, 2006.

Mabee, Bryan. "Pirates, Privateers, and the Political Economy of Pirate Violence." *Global Change, Peace & Security* 21 (2009): 139–52.

Malekandathil, Pius. "From Merchant Capitalists to Corsairs: The Response of the Muslim Merchants of Malabar to the Portuguese Commercial Expansion, 1498–1600." *Portuguese Studies Review* 12 (2004): 75–96.

Marley, David F. *Pirates of the Americas.* 2 vols. Santa Barbara: ABC-CLIO, 2010.

———. *Sack of Veracruz: The Great Pirate Raid of 1683.* Windsor, ON: Netherlandic Press, 1993.

Marx, Jenifer. *Pirates and Privateers of the Caribbean.* Malabar, FL: Krieger, 1992.

Marx, Robert. *Pirate Port: The Story of the Sunken City of Port Royal.* Cleveland: World, 1967.

Matar, Nabil. *Britain and Barbary, 1589–1689.* Gainesville: University Press of Florida, 2006.

Matta Rodríguez-Caso, Enrique de la. *El asalto de Pointis a Cartagena de Indias.* Sevilla: Escuela de Estudios Hispano-Americanos, 1979.

McCarl, Clayton, ed. *Piratas y contrabandistas de ambas Indias, y estado presente de ellas (1693), por Francisco Seyxas y Lovera.* La Coruña: Fundación Pedro Barrié de la Maza, 2011.

McCarthy, Matthew. *Privateering, Piracy and British Policy in Spanish America, 1810–1830.* Woodbridge: Boydell, 2013.

McDermott, James. *Martin Frobisher, Elizabethan Privateer.* New Haven: Yale University Press, 2001.

McDonald, Kevin P. *Pirates, Merchants, Settlers, and Slaves: Colonial America and the Indo-Atlantic World.* Berkeley: University of California Press, 2015.

Merrien, Jean. *Histoire des corsaires.* Saint-Malo: Editions l'Ancre de marine, 1992.

Montero, Pablo. *Imperios y piratas.* Mexico City: Editorial Porrúa, 2003.

Moore, David. "Blackbeard the Pirate: Historical Background and the Beaufort Inlet Shipwrecks." *Tributaries* 7 (1997): 31–39.

Moreau, Jean-Pierre. *Pirates: flibuste et piraterie dans la Caraïbe et les mers du Sud, 1522–1725.* Paris: Tallandier, 2006.

Neill, Anna. "Buccaneer Ethnography: Nature, Culture, and Nation in the Journals of William Dampier." *Eighteenth-Century Studies* 33 (2000): 165–80.

Nerzic, Jean-Yves, and Christian Buchet. *Marins et flibustiers du Roi-Soleil: Carthagène, 1697.* Aspet: PyréGraph, 2002.

Olivié, Frantz, and Raynald Laprise. *L'enfer de la flibuste.* Toulouse: Anacharsis, 2016.

Parry, John H. *The Age of Reconnaissance.* New York: Mentor Books, 1963.

Pawson, Michael, and David Buisseret. *Port Royal, Jamaica.* Oxford: Clarendon Press, 1975.

Pelúcia, Alexandra. *Corsários e piratas portugueses: Aventureiros nos mares da Ásia.* Lisbon: A Esfera dos Livros, 2010.

Pennell, C. Richard, ed. *Bandits at Sea: A Pirates Reader.* New York: New York University Press, 2001.

Pérez Mejía, Angela. "Fronteras de la legalidad: Bucaneros en el siglo XVII." *Historia y sociedad* 8 (2002): 179–98.

Pérotin-Dumon, Anne. "The Pirate and the Emperor: Power and Law on the Seas, 1450–1850," In *The Political Economy of Merchant Empires: State, Power, and World Trade, 1350–1750*, edited by James D. Tracy, 169–227. Cambridge: Cambridge University Press, 1991.

Pestana, Carla Gardina. *The Conquest of Jamaica: Oliver Cromwell's Bid for Empire*. Cambridge, MA: Harvard University Press, 2017.

———. "Early English Jamaica without Pirates." *The William and Mary Quarterly* 71 (2014): 321–60.

Petrovich, Sandra. *Henry Morgan's Raid on Panama: Geopolitics and Colonial Ramifications, 1669–1674*. Lewiston, NY: Edwin Mellen Press, 2001.

Phillips, Carla Rahn. *Six Galleons for the King of Spain: Imperial Defense in the Early Seventeenth Century*. Baltimore: Johns Hopkins University Press, 1986.

Poolman, Kenneth. *The* Speedwell *Voyage: A Tale of Piracy and Mutiny in the Eighteenth Century*. Annapolis: Naval Institute Press, 1999.

Prange, Sebastian R. "A Trade of No Dishonor: Piracy, Commerce, and Community in the Western Indian Ocean, Twelfth to Sixteenth Century." *American Historical Review* 116 (2011): 1269–93.

Preston, Diana, and Michael. *A Pirate of Exquisite Mind: Explorer, Naturalist, and Buccaneer: The Life of William Dampier*. New York: Berkeley, 2004.

Ramírez Aznar, Luis A. *De piratas y corsarios: La piratería en la península de Yucatán*. Mérida: Universidad Autónoma de Yucatán, 2001.

Rankin, Hugh F. *The Golden Age of Piracy*. New York: Holt, Rinehart, 1969.

Rediker, Marcus. *Between the Devil and the Deep Blue Sea: Merchant Seamen, Pirates, and the Anglo-American Maritime World, 1700–1750*. New York: Cambridge University Press, 1987.

———. *Villains of All Nations: Atlantic Pirates in the Golden Age*. Boston: Beacon Press, 2004.

Rennie, Neil. *Treasure Neverland: Real and Imaginary Pirates*. Oxford: Oxford University Press, 2013.

Requemora, Sylvie, and Sophie Linon-Chipon, eds. *Les Tyrans de la mer: pirates, corsaires et flibustiers*. Paris: Presses de l'Université de Paris-Sorbonne, 2002.

Risso, Patricia. "Cross-Cultural Perceptions of Piracy: Maritime Violence in the Western Indian Ocean and Persian Gulf during a Long Eighteenth Century." *Journal of World History* 12 (2001): 293–319.

Ritchie, Robert C. *Captain Kidd and the War against the Pirates*. Cambridge, MA: Harvard University Press, 1986.

Roberts, Nancy. *Blackbeard and Other Pirates of the Atlantic Coast*. Winston-Salem, NC: John F. Blair, 1993.

Rodger, N. A. M. "The Law and Language of Private Naval Warfare." *Mariner's Mirror* 100 (February 2014): 5–16.

Rogers, Woodes. *A Cruising Voyage Round the World*. New York: Dover, 1970.

Rogoziński, Jan. *Pirates! Brigands, Buccaneers, and Privateers in Fact, Fiction, and Legend*. New York: DaCapo, 1996.

Rubin, Alfred P. *The Law of Piracy*. Newport, RI: Naval War College Press, 1988.

Ruiz Gil, Helena, and Francisco Morales Padrón. *Piratería en el Caribe*. Sevilla: Editorial Renamiciento, 2005.

Sáiz Cidoncha, Carlos. *Historia de la piratería en América española*. Madrid: San Martín, 1985.

Serrano Mangas, Fernando. "Auge y represión de la piratería en el Caribe, 1650–1700." *Mesoamérica* 6 (1985): 91–103.

Shomette, Donald G. *Pirates of the Chesapeake: Being a True History of Pirates, Picaroons, and Raiders on Chesapeake Bay, 1610–1807*. Centreville, MD: Tidewater, 1985.

Skowronek, Russell K., and Charles R. Ewen, eds. *X Marks the Spot: The Archaeology of Piracy*. Gainesville: University Press of Florida, 2006.

Snelders, Stephen. "Chirurgijns onder zeerovers in de 17e eeuw." *Nederlands Tijdschrift voor de Geneeskunde* 24 (2005): 2933–36.

So, Kwan-Wai. *Japanese Piracy in Ming China during the 16th Century*. Ann Arbor: University of Michigan Press, 1975.

Sousa, Philip de. *Piracy in the Graeco-Roman World*. New York: Cambridge University Press, 2002.

Spinelli, Anna. *Tra l'inferno e il mare: Breve storia economica e sociale della pirateria*. Ravenna: Fernandel, 2003.

Starkey, David J., Elisabeth S. van Eyck van Heslinga, Jaap A. de Moor, eds. *Pirates and Privateers: New Perspectives in the War on Trade in the Eighteenth and Nineteenth Centuries*. Exeter: University of Exeter Press, 1997.

Subramanian, Lakshmi. *The Sovereign and the Pirate: Ordering Maritime Subjects in India's Western Littoral*. New York: Oxford University Press, 2016.

Sugden, John. *Sir Francis Drake*. New York: Henry Holt, 1992.

Thompson, Janice E. *Mercenaries, Pirates, and Sovereigns: State-building and Extraterritorial Violence in Early Modern Europe*. Princeton: Princeton University Press, 1994.

Thrower, Norman J., ed. *Sir Francis Drake and the Famous Voyage, 1577–1580: Essays Commemorating the Quadricentennial of Drake's Circumnavigation of the World*. Berkeley: University of California Press, 1984.

Tinniswood, Adrian. *Pirates of Barbary: Corsairs, Conquests, and Captivity in the Seventeenth-Century Mediterranean*. New York: Riverhead Books, 2010.

Valenzuela Solís de Ovando, Carlos. *Piratas en el Pacífico*. Santiago: La Noria, 1993.

Victoria Ojeda, Jorge. "La piratería y su relación con los indígenas de la península de Yucatán: Mito y práctica social." *Mesoamérica* 14 (1993): 209–16.

———. *Piratas en Yucatán*. Mérida: Editorial Area Maya, 2007.

Vitkus, Daniel J. *Piracy, Slavery, and Redemption.* New York: Columbia University Press, 2001.

Warren, James F. *Iranun and Balangingi: Globalization, Maritime Raiding, and the Birth of Ethnicity.* Singapore: National University of Singapore Press, 2002.

Weiss, Gillian. *Captives and Corsairs: France and Slavery in the Early Modern Mediterranean.* Stanford: Stanford University Press, 2011.

Wilbur, Marguerite E. *Raveneau de Lussan: Buccaneer of the Spanish Main and Early French Filibuster of the Pacific.* Cleveland: Arthur H. Clark, 1930.

Williams, Daniel E. "Puritans and Pirates: A Confrontation between Cotton Mather and William Fly in 1726." *Early American Literature* 22 (1987): 233–51.

Wilson, David. "From the Caribbean to Craignish: Imperial Authority and Piratical Voyages in the Early Eighteenth-Century Atlantic Commons." *Itinerario* 42 (2018): 430–60.

Woodard, Colin. *The Republic of Pirates: Being the True and Surprising Story of the Caribbean Pirates and the Man Who Brought them Down.* New York: Harcourt, 2007.

Zahedieh, Nuala. "'A Frugal, Prudential and Hopeful Trade': Privateering in Jamaica, 1655–1689." *Journal of Imperial and Commonwealth History* 18 (1990): 145–68.

INDEX